ARTS and CRAFTS
for ALL SEASONS

www.themailbox.com

The Education Center®

Arts and Crafts for All Seasons
Primary—Grades 1–3: TEC927

Created for The Education Center, Inc., by
Two-Can Publishing Ltd., 346 Old Street,
London EC1V 9RB, U.K.

Craft authors
Melanie Williams
Claire Watts
Dawn Apperley
Marian Bright
Deri Robins

Illustrators
Kelly Dooley
Jo Moore
Claire Boyce
Michael Evans
Sonia Canals

www.themailbox.com

Published © 1999 by THE EDUCATION CENTER, INC.
All rights reserved
ISBN# 1-56234-206-1

Manufactured in the United States
10 9 8 7 6 5 4 3

Contents

Art Tips

About This Book

● For each project, materials are listed in quantities for one child. Simply multiply the quantities given by the number of children in your class to work out your exact requirements. There are several shared projects, such as Day-By-Day Calendar (page 10). In these cases, the group quantities are clearly stated.

● To save time and avoid waste, most projects use standard paper sizes, or sizes that can be easily cut from them. All other materials are standard sizes unless stated. The glue used is ordinary white school glue.

● A section called "Class Preparations" is included for projects which require simple pre-lesson preparations. These sometimes involve making templates for the children to share. Provide one template for every two children in the class, unless otherwise stated.

● Some projects include patterns to duplicate. The easiest method of copying onto tagboard or construction paper is to use a photocopier. Alternatively, trace a pattern, cut out the shape, and use it as a template to trace the shape onto individual sheets of paper.

● Step-by-step directions guide you through every stage of the project. An ⓗ symbol indicates that the children may need particular help at this step. The ⓣ symbol indicates that you will need to carry out the step yourself.

● All the projects are simple and easy to make but it's a good idea to try them out first: you'll understand them fully and have a sample to show the class. For more complicated projects, such as Woven Hearts (page 80), make your own artwork along with the class, to demonstrate each stage.

Collecting Materials

● At the start of the year, send the children home with a duplicated letter requesting scrap materials. Write your own or copy the letter on page 6. Check the items you need, add others not on the list, and sign your name. Repeat the letter whenever supplies are running low or you need a specific item.

● When requesting a specific item, such as a photograph for Shell Frame (page 129), write the date that the item is needed, give the dimensions if important, and remember to give out the letter well in advance.

● Think ahead—have children bring in used cards and gift wrap after Christmas, Easter, and other celebrations. You may not need them right away, but they're sure to come in handy in the future.

Practical Tips

● When children use scissors or a pencil to make a hole, or cut out a shape to leave a frame, have them push the scissors or pencil through the paper into a piece of modeling clay on the other side.

● Why not turn your students' artwork into protective mats for their desks? Cut a large piece of tagboard for each child; then have the children paint a picture and label it with their name. Cover both sides of the paper with Con-Tact® paper to make a wipe-clean painting mat.

● To make a large, waterproof table cover, cut down one side and across the bottom of a large plastic garbage bag; then tape onto the table.

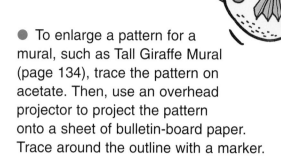

● To enlarge a pattern for a mural, such as Tall Giraffe Mural (page 134), trace the pattern on acetate. Then, use an overhead projector to project the pattern onto a sheet of bulletin-board paper. Trace around the outline with a marker.

● Use tempera paints on unwaxed paper cups and plates. Try mixing paint with a little glue to help it stick or to create a glazed effect.

Displaying Craft Projects

● Hang a clothesline across your classroom and use clothespins for hanging artwork. It's a useful way to dry paintings, too.

● Display long artwork, such as Leaf Chain (page 19), as a bulletin-board trim or as a decoration around the edges of the chalkboard.

● On a breezy spring day, have your students paint a picture, such as Seaside Print (page 112), on fabric. Then tie the artwork to a tree and watch it flutter in the wind.

Techniques and Recipes

● Accordion-folding
Use this technique for pop-up features or to make bulletin-board trims, such as Halloween Cats (page 24). Fold a small flap upward at one end of a piece of paper. Turn the paper over and fold the double flap backward, to the same width as before. Continue to the end of the paper.

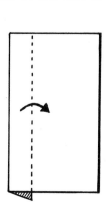
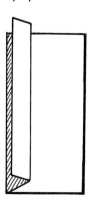
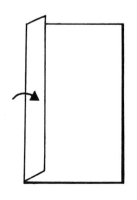

● Salt Dough
Use this as an alternative to self-hardening modeling clay. Mix two cups of flour and one cup of salt in a bowl. Slowly mix in a cup of water. Knead the dough well until it is no longer sticky. Keep the dough in a plastic bag so that it doesn't dry out. It will last about five days. To harden the dough, either leave it in a warm place for two to three days, or bake it in a 300°F oven for about an hour.

● Papier Mâché
To make a paste, sift five cups of flour into a container, then add one cup of water and mix well. Add more water slowly until the paste is the consistency of thick cream. Dip strips of newspaper in the paste, or watered-down glue, to make papier mâché.

Dear Parent

Can you help us collect some art supplies? Most of these items are things you would usually throw away. Please clean them out, save them, and send them to school with your child.

We need the items checked below:

❑ candle stubs
❑ cardboard cartons
❑ glass jars
❑ liquid detergent bottles
❑ plastic bottles
❑ yogurt containers
❑ plastic drinking straws
❑ cardboard tubes
❑ aluminum foil
❑ Styrofoam® dishes
❑ paper cups
❑ paper plates

❑ aluminum foil dishes
❑ Styrofoam® packing material
❑ bubble wrap
❑ fabric scraps
❑ yarn
❑ ribbon
❑ buttons
❑ newspapers
❑ magazines and catalogs
❑ gift wrap
❑ old greetings cards
❑ sponges
❑ clothespins

Others

❑ _____

❑ _____

❑ _____

Thank you!

Here are some great ways to help children in your class get to know each other at the start of the year.

Fall Harvest

• • • • • • • • • • • • • • • •

Materials For Each Group:
1 sheet of 12" x 18" construction paper, with letter outline
fall collage materials, such as leaves, twigs, and nuts
scissors and glue

Class Preparations:
Organize the children into four groups. Have each group make a collection of different fall collage materials such as leaves, twigs, and nuts, as well as harvest produce such as wheat, lentils, and rice. Draw each letter in the word "FALL" on a separate sheet of construction paper. Then, have each group decorate one of the letters.

Directions:
1. Cut out the letter.
2. Glue on the various collage materials that your group has collected, to cover the letter.
3. Display with other letters on a bulletin board. 🌕

Name Cards

• • • • • • • • • • • • • • • •

Materials For Each Child:
1/4 sheet of 9" x 12" colored construction paper
old magazines to share
scissors and glue

Class Preparations:
For each child, cut a piece of 4 1/2" x 6" colored construction paper.

Directions:
1. Fold the paper in half lengthwise.
2. Cut out from old magazines the letters that make up your name. Try to find letters in a variety of sizes, styles, and colors.
3. Arrange the letters on one side of the paper and glue them in position.
4. Stand up your name card to show everyone your name.

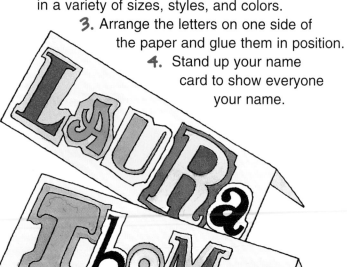

Schultutes are traditional German candy cones. Treat your youngsters with these first-day-at-school gifts!

Schultute

• • • • • • • • • • • • • •

Materials For Each Child:
1 square of yellow construction paper, 12" x 12"
1 strip of orange crepe paper or tissue paper,
  18" x 6"
1 ribbon, 12" in length
small candies
colored markers, tape, and glue

Class Preparations:
For each child, cut a curve from corner to corner of the construction-paper square, as shown (A).

Directions:
1. Use colored markers to decorate one side of the construction paper.
2. Turn over the construction paper and glue a crepe-paper or tissue-paper strip across the curved edge (B). Allow to dry. ✋
3. Curl the construction paper into a cone and glue together the overlapping edges. Secure with tape around the rim on the inside. ✋
4. Fill the cone with candies; then use a ribbon to tie the crepe paper or tissue paper closed. ✋

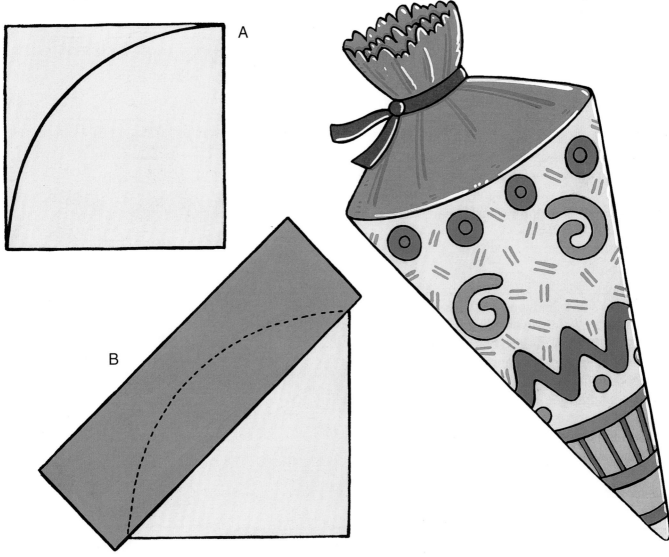

A

B

Day-By-Day Calendar

DAY   MONTH   DATE   WEATHER

Materials For The Whole Class:
14 sheets of 9" x 12" construction paper,
    in a variety of colors
1 piece of 9" x 25" bulletin-board paper
4 large manila envelopes
4 large paper clips
collage materials, such as paper and
    fabric scraps
tempera paints and paintbrushes
colored markers, scissors, and glue

Class Preparations:
For this class project, make the calendar
background by cutting a 9" x 25" piece of
bulletin-board paper and label it "DAY",
"MONTH", "DATE", and "WEATHER", as shown.
Label four large envelopes to match and have
four large paper clips ready.

Have the whole class work together to make
56 decorated calendar cards, to represent
seven days of the week, 12 months, 31 days,
and six types of weather—sunny, rainy, windy,
cloudy, snowy, and stormy. Assign cards to
each child in the class.

Directions:
1. To make four cards, fold a sheet of paper
into quarters and cut along the folds.
2. Write a day of the week, month, number,
or type of weather on each one of the cards. Ⓗ
3. Use markers, paints, and collage materials
to decorate the card with appropriate symbols.
4. Repeat until you have made all your
assigned calendar cards. Ⓗ
5. Sort the cards into the four envelopes and
store these by the calendar.
6. Each day, use paper clips to attach the
relevant day, month, date, and weather to the
calendar background. Ⓣ

Pencil Pot

Materials For Each Child:

1 piece of thick white string, 30' in length
1 glass jar
old magazines and comics, to share
newspaper
runny tempera paints in shallow containers
scissors
glue

Class Preparations:

Mix tempera paints with water to make them very runny and pour into shallow containers.

Directions:

1. Dip sections of the string in different colors of paint, to make the string multi-colored. Lay on newspaper to dry.

2. Cover the lower part of the jar with glue.

3. Wrap the string tightly around the jar, starting at the bottom. Keep the layers close together and apply more glue as necessary. ⏁

4. When you reach the top of the jar, cut the string and glue the end down neatly.

5. Cut out a favorite cartoon figure from a magazine or comic and glue it to the jar, if desired.

Back-To-School Pencil Caddy

Materials For Each Child:

1 aluminum can, covered in red or yellow Con-Tact® paper
1/3 sheet each of 9" x 12" red, orange, and yellow construction paper
variety of leaves
pencil, scissors
paintbrush and watered-down glue

Class Preparations:

Have your class make a collection of fall leaves in different shapes and sizes. Collect clean, empty food cans and cover them with red or yellow Con-Tact® paper. Cut sheets of construction paper into thirds and provide each child with three different-colored pieces.

Directions:

1. Draw around a leaf on a piece of paper and cut out the shape. Continue making paper leaves until you have used up all three pieces of paper.

2. Glue paper leaves on the can. Allow to dry.

3. Brush over the whole can with glue to seal.

Before you try these projects, discuss with your students how different foods are harvested.

Growing Corn

Materials For Each Group:
1 sheet of 9" x 12" yellow construction paper, with 5 corn-cob outlines
1 sheet of 12" x 18" yellow tissue paper
4 sheets of green bulletin-board paper
ruler, scissors, and glue

Class Preparations:
Have children work in groups of five. For each group, duplicate the corn-cob pattern below five times on yellow construction paper.

Directions:
1. Stack the sheets of green bulletin-board paper; then roll the sheets up lengthwise and tape the long edge.
2. Cut four slits, 6" long, around the top of the paper roll. Gently pull up the inside rolls of paper so that the paper resembles a tall plant. Cut the slits in the outer layers to make them slightly longer.
3. Cut out the corn cobs. Tear tissue paper into small pieces and crumple into balls. Glue all over the corn cobs.
4. Glue the corn cobs onto the plant, as shown.

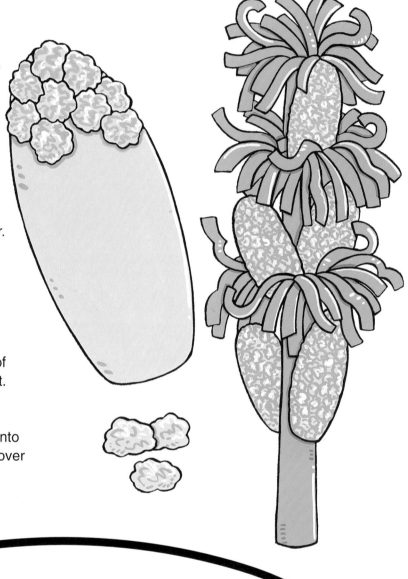

Finger Vegetable Fields

Materials For Each Child:
1 sheet of 9" x 12" light green construction paper
construction-paper scraps
green, white, brown, and orange tempera paints
  in shallow dishes
paintbrush
pencil and ruler

Class Preparations:
Provide pictures of vegetables growing in fields.

Directions:
1. First, use a pencil and ruler to divide a sheet of construction paper into four sections, as shown. These are your fields.

2. Before making your vegetable prints for real, practice on construction-paper scraps. To make cabbage prints, curve your little finger and dip the side of it in green paint. Press down firmly on paper. When you have made a good, neat print, make several rows of cabbage prints in one of your vegetable fields. Then wash your hands.

3. Repeat step 2 for different types of vegetables. Make white thumbprints for potatoes; use the side of your fist for an orange pumpkin; and use the whole length of your little finger for orange carrots. Fill each field with a different vegetable.

4. Add green stalks with a paintbrush.

5. Finally, add brown fingerprints around the vegetables for soil.

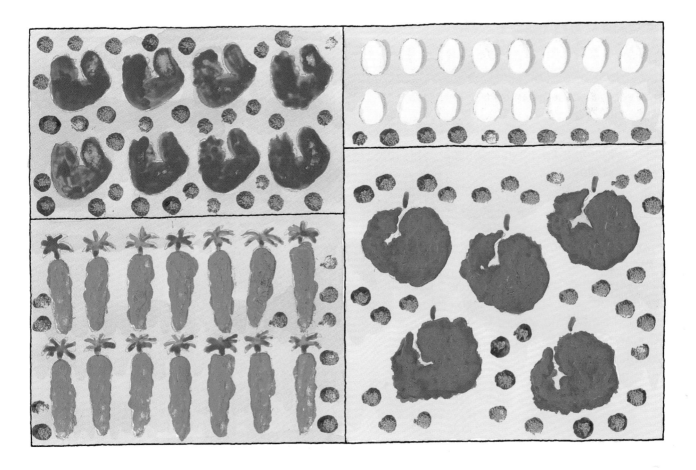

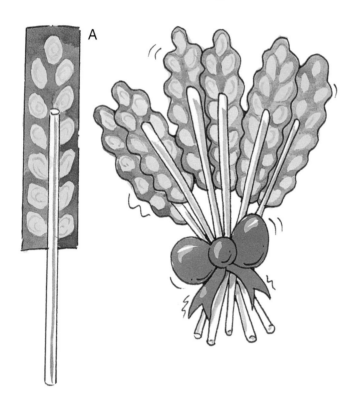

A

Wheat Sheaf

Materials For Each Child:
6 brown construction-paper strips, 6" x 1½"
6 plain white straws
1 orange ribbon, 12" in length
corn-yellow tempera paint in a shallow container
scissors and glue

Directions:
1. Glue one end of each straw onto the center of a construction-paper strip, as shown. Allow to dry.
2. Dip your index finger in corn-yellow paint and make fingerprints on the construction paper, down each side of the straw (A). Allow to dry.
3. Cut around the edges of the fingerprints to make wheat ears.
4. Arrange the wheat ears in a fan shape and tie with a ribbon to make a sheaf. Ⓗ

Harvest Festival Food

Materials For Each Child:
several sheets of newspaper
green construction-paper scrap
a small twig
tempera paints and paintbrushes
masking tape, scissors, water, and glue

Directions:
1. Crumple a sheet of newspaper into the shape of a fruit. Wrap masking tape around the fruit to keep it in shape. Ⓗ
2. Tear another sheet of newspaper into strips and glue them on the fruit to cover it. Allow to dry overnight.
3. Add a second layer of strips and allow to dry.
4. Push a twig into the fruit for a stalk. Paint the fruit all over and allow to dry.
5. Mix equal parts of glue and water in a plastic container. Ⓣ
6. Brush the watered-down glue all over the fruit to add some shine; then cut out a green construction-paper leaf and glue it to the top.

Crunchy Apple Stationery

Materials For Each Child:

1 sheet of letter-writing paper and 1 envelope
1 whole-apple template, to share
1 bitten-apple template, to share
2 sponge pieces, about 3" x 3" and
 no thicker than 1½"
2 posterboard squares, 3" x 3"
construction-paper scraps
dark green and light green tempera paints
 in shallow containers
brown marker
scissors and glue

Class Preparations:

Use the patterns below to make whole-apple and bitten-apple templates for the children to share.

Directions:

1. Trace each template on a piece of sponge and cut out. Glue each sponge apple on a posterboard square to make a printing block.
2. Practice printing on paper scraps. Dip the whole-apple printing block in light green paint and print. Dip the bitten-apple printing block in dark green paint and print exactly on top of the first print.
3. When you have made a good, neat print, repeat on the top left-hand corner of a sheet of letter-writing paper. Print another apple on the top left-hand corner of an envelope.
4. Use a marker to draw a stalk on each apple.

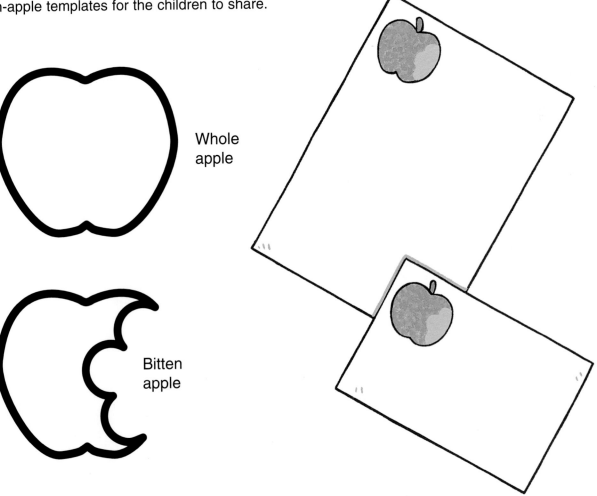

Whole
apple

Bitten
apple

15

Quilled Apple Orchard

Materials For Each Child:
1 sheet of 9" x 12" green construction paper,
   with 2 tree-top outlines
1/2 sheet of 9" x 12" green construction paper
1/2 sheet of 9" x 12" brown construction paper
1/4 sheet of 9" x 12" red construction paper
green Styrofoam® trays, to share
a ball of green modeling clay
scissors, ruler, pencil, and glue

Class Preparations:
For this group project, duplicate the tree-top
pattern on the opposite page twice on a sheet
of green construction paper for each child.
Have several green Styrofoam® trays ready
for displaying the children's trees.

Directions:
1. Cut out the two tree-top shapes. Cut red
construction paper and the rest of the green
paper into strips about 1/4" x 2". 🄷
2. Wrap each paper strip tightly around
a pencil to curl it (A). 🄷
3. Spread glue on
the tree-tops and
stick down red
curls for
apples and
green curls
for leaves.

4. Roll up the brown construction paper tightly
widthwise and glue along the edge to make a
trunk. Dip one end in glue, then sandwich the
trunk between the two tree-tops (B). Allow to dry.
5. Push the base of the trunk into a ball of
modeling clay.
6. Arrange several trees in a Styrofoam® tray
to create an orchard. 🅃

A

B

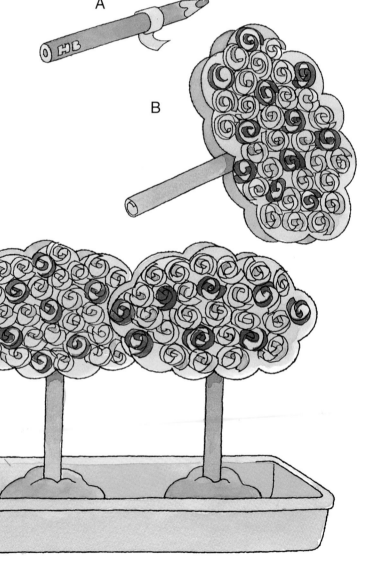

A Harvest Of Good Work

Materials For The Whole Class:
1 large piece of bulletin-board paper
vegetables and fruits for printing, such as
   apples, cauliflower florets, cabbages,
   peppers, carrots, and broccoli spears
tempera paints in saucers

Class Preparations:
For this group project, cut vegetables and fruits
into halves or quarters. Have a stapler and a
black marker ready. Invite children to take it in
turns to make a print on the paper.

Directions:
1. Dip the flat side of a fruit or vegetable piece
into paint and print carefully near the edge of the
bulletin-board paper.
2. Use another fruit or vegetable to make a
different-colored print next to the first one.

3. Continue printing together to make a border
around the paper. Allow to dry.
4. Staple the paper to the bulletin board. Use a
black marker to add the title "A Harvest Of Good
Work" and use the space inside the printed border
to display students' papers. Ⓣ

Use with Quilled Apple
Orchard on page 16.

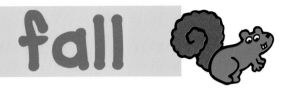
Red Apple Place Card

Materials For Each Child:
1 sheet of 9" x 12" light green construction paper
1/4 sheet of 9" x 12" red construction paper
1 apple template, to share
light green construction-paper scraps
dark-colored crayon
black marker
pencil, scissors, and glue

Class Preparations:
Use the pattern on the right to make apple templates for the children to share. Cut a piece of 4 1/2" x 6" red construction paper for each child.

Directions:
1. Use the template to trace and cut out an apple from red construction paper. Use a black marker to color the stalk.
2. Cut out two simple leaf shapes from light green construction paper. Use a dark-colored crayon to draw veins on each of them.
3. Glue the leaves on your apple.
4. Fold a sheet of green paper in half to make a place card. Glue your paper apple to the top of the card, as shown. Allow to dry.
5. Write your name on the place card.

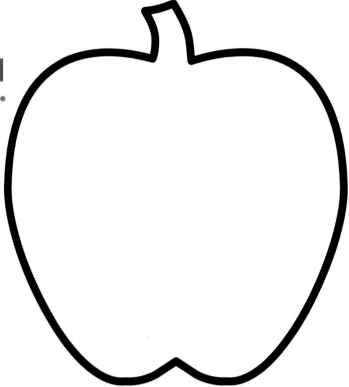

Use with Red Apple Place Card on this page.

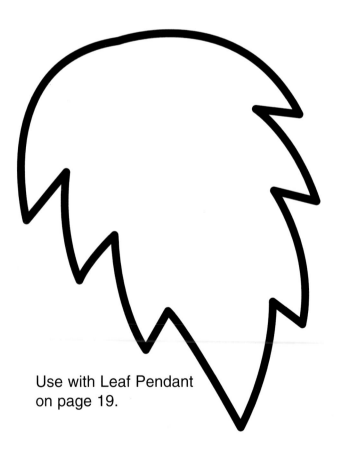

Use with Leaf Pendant on page 19.

Have your students collect fallen leaves for these projects. Remind them to look out for squirrels!

Leaf Pendant

· · · · · · · · · · · · · · · · · ·

Materials For Each Child:
1/2 sheet of 9" x 12" construction paper
1 leaf template, to share
1 piece of narrow ribbon, 20" in length
1 paper clip
tissue-paper scraps in fall colors
string, paintbrush, scissors, and glue

Class Preparations:
Use the pattern on page 18 to make leaf templates for children to share.

Directions:
1. Trace and cut out two paper leaves.
2. Spread glue over one leaf. Lay a paper clip on the glued side so that one end of the clip sticks out. Lay the other leaf on top, making sure the edges of both leaves match exactly. Press firmly together.
3. Cut short lengths of string and glue to one side to resemble veins. Allow to dry.
4. Tear tissue paper into small pieces and glue two layers over the back of the pendant. Allow to dry; then repeat on the front. Press around the veins with the end of a paintbrush (A).
5. When dry, paint the leaf with glue.
6. Thread a ribbon through the paper clip and tie the ends. (H)

Leaf Chain

· · · · · · · · · · · · · · · ·

Materials For Each Child:
10 leaves, all different shapes and colors
1 piece of narrow ribbon, 20" in length
hole puncher to share
newspaper
watered-down glue
paintbrush

Class Preparations:
Mix equal parts of glue and water in plastic containers. Have a stapler ready.

Directions:
1. Lay each leaf on newspaper and brush watered-down glue all over one side. Carefully lift up each leaf and place it glue-side up on a clean sheet of newspaper to dry.
2. When dry, turn the leaves over and varnish the other side of each one in the same way.
3. Use a hole puncher to punch a hole near one end of each leaf and thread ribbon through all the holes. (H)
4. Tie a knot in each end of your ribbon, or help tie everybody's ribbons together to make one long class chain. (H)
5. Staple to the bulletin board. (T)

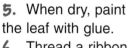
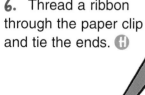
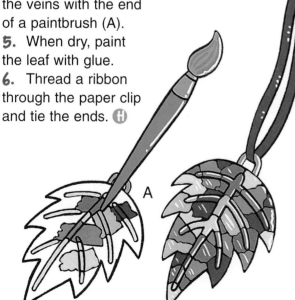

A

fall

Fall Frame

Materials For Each Child:
1 cardboard frame, about 6" x 6"
1/6 sheet of 9" x 12" construction paper
1 posterboard triangle
1 photo or drawing, 3" x 3" or larger
blue, green, red, yellow, and orange
  tissue paper
paintbrush
scissors and watered-down glue

Class Preparations:
To make a frame for each child, use a craft knife to cut a 3" square from the middle of a piece of cardboard. Frames can be square, oval, or free form. To make a stand for each frame, cut a 3" posterboard square, then halve this diagonally to make a triangle. Also cut a 4" x 4 1/2" piece of construction paper to cover the back of each frame. Mix equal parts of glue and water.

A

Directions:
1. Tear blue or green tissue paper into squares or irregular shapes. Glue two layers all over the frame and allow to dry overnight.
2. Cut fall shapes such as acorns, leaves, or apples from tissue paper and glue to the frame.
3. Spread glue on the bottom and side edges of your piece of construction paper and fix to the back of the frame to cover the hole. Allow to dry; then slide in a photo or picture. ⓗ
4. To make a stand for your frame, fold over one edge of the posterboard triangle and glue to the back of the frame (A). ⓗ

Twiggy Creatures

Materials For Each Child:
1 twig
tempera paints
paintbrushes

Class Preparations:
Have the children collect twigs with interesting shapes.

Directions:
1. Think about the shape of your twig. What do you think it looks like? Use your imagination, and see if you can find a head, legs, and a tail.
2. Paint on features in lots of different colors to turn your twig into a wonderful creature!

Squirrel Hideout

• •

Materials For Each Child:
1 sheet of 9" x 12" light brown
    construction paper
1 square of black construction paper, 6" x 6"
½ sheet of 9" x 12" red construction paper,
    with squirrel outline
tempera paints in fall colors
paintbrushes
pencil and ruler
scissors, tape, and glue

Class Preparations:
For each child, duplicate the squirrel pattern
below on red construction paper.

Directions:
1. Draw a large tree-trunk shape on
brown construction paper and cut out.
2. Paint a bark design on the trunk.
Allow to dry.
3. Turn over the trunk and use a
pencil to draw the outline of a round
door, approximately 5" in diameter.
Push scissors through the paper
at the top of the door outline
(see Practical Tips, page 4). Then
cut along the line, leaving a hinge
on one side.
4. Cover the opening with the
black construction-paper square;
then tape down.
5. Turn over the trunk and open
the door. Cut out the squirrel and
glue on the black paper.

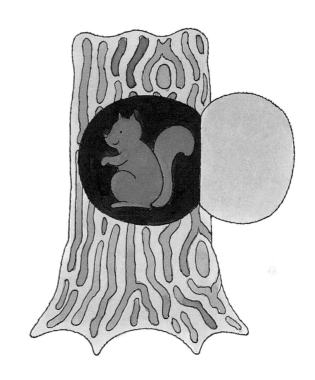

fall

A

Fall Pixie Hats

Materials For Each Child:
3 sheets of 9" x 12" white drawing paper
1 paper plate, 10" in diameter
1 piece of elastic, 8" in length
several different-shaped leaves
stapler to share
wax crayons in fall colors, scissors, and glue

Class Preparations:
Ask your class to collect a variety of leaves.

Directions:
1. To make leaf rubbings, lay a piece of drawing paper over the veined side of a leaf and gently rub with a crayon. Repeat with different leaves and colors. Cut out the leaf rubbings.
2. Make a straight cut from the edge of your plate to the center. Overlap the edges to make a cone hat. (H)
3. Staple the edges in place; then staple one end of a length of elastic to each side of the hat. (H)
4. Starting at the base of the hat, glue on paper leaves in overlapping layers (A), until the hat is covered.

Day And Night Faces

Materials For Each Child:
2 paper plates, 7" in diameter
2 craft sticks
1 star template, to share
orange and yellow yarn
Styrofoam® meat tray
yellow, black, and dark blue tempera paints
silver paint in a small dish
paintbrushes, pencil, scissors, and glue

Class Preparations:
Use the pattern on page 29 to make star templates for the children to share.

Directions:
1. To make the sun's face, paint the back of one plate yellow. Allow to dry; then paint on black eyes and a mouth. Cut yarn into small pieces and glue around the face to make rays.
2. Paint a silver crescent moon and dark blue sky on the back of the other plate. Allow to dry.
3. Use the template to trace and cut out a Styrofoam® star. Glue to the blunt end of a pencil and use to print silver stars in the sky. Paint a black eye on the moon and allow to dry.
4. Turn both plates over and spread glue around the rims. Place two craft sticks on opposite sides of one plate for handles. Press the glued edges of the plates together; then allow to dry.
5. Twist the craft sticks to flip from day to night.

Your students will love to make ghoulish classroom decorations at Halloween. These projects are ideal!

Spooky Wind Chimes

Materials For Each Child:
1 colored plastic cup
6 pieces of colored plastic cutlery
1 piece of string, 4' in length
Halloween stickers
scissors, ruler, and tape

Class Preparations:
Use one of the points on a pair of sharp scissors to make a hole in the bottom of each child's cup (see Practical Tips, page 4).

Directions:
1. Decorate the cup with Halloween stickers.
2. Cut a 12" length from your string. Tie a double knot in one end and thread the string through the hole in the cup from the inside. (H)
3. Cut the remaining string into six different lengths.
4. Tape one end of each length of string to a piece of cutlery. Tape the other end of each string to the inside of the cup.
5. Hang the wind chimes by an open window or door where they will make a spooky noise. (H)

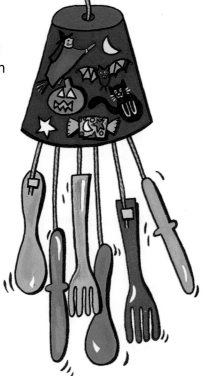

Jumping Black Cat

Materials For Each Child:
½ sheet of 9" x 12" orange construction paper
¼ sheet of 9" x 12" black construction paper
1 cat template, to share
1 strip of posterboard, 3" x 1"
2 wiggle eyes
pink and white tempera paints
paintbrushes, pencil, scissors, and glue

Class Preparations:
Use the pattern on page 24 to make several cat templates for children to share. For each child, cut a piece of 9" x 6" orange construction paper and a piece of 4½" x 6" black construction paper. Also cut a strip of posterboard, measuring 3" x 1".

Directions:
1. Fold the orange paper in half to make a card.
2. Trace and cut out a cat from black paper.
3. Glue on wiggle eyes. Paint on white whiskers, a pink nose, and a pink mouth.
4. Fold the posterboard strip in thirds along its length and glue one end to the orange card (A). Glue the other end to the cat. (H)

Halloween Cats

. . . .

Materials For Each Child:
½ sheet of 12" x 18" black construction paper
1 cat template
green glitter
pencil and ruler
scissors and glue

Class Preparations:
For each child, use the pattern below to make a cat template, and cut a 6" x 18" piece of black construction paper.

Directions:
1. Use a ruler and pencil to divide the construction paper into four sections, each 4½" wide. Accordion-fold the paper along the lines. **ⓗ**
2. Trace the cat template onto the top section of the paper (A) and cut out the shape. Do not cut along the folds, shown by the dotted lines.
3. Unfold the paper. Spread glue on each cat's feet and put two dots of glue on each cat's face for eyes. Sprinkle on green glitter. Allow to dry.
4. Pin all the cats in a long line on the bulletin board. **ⓣ**

A

Use with Jumping Black Cat on page 23 and Halloween Cats on this page.

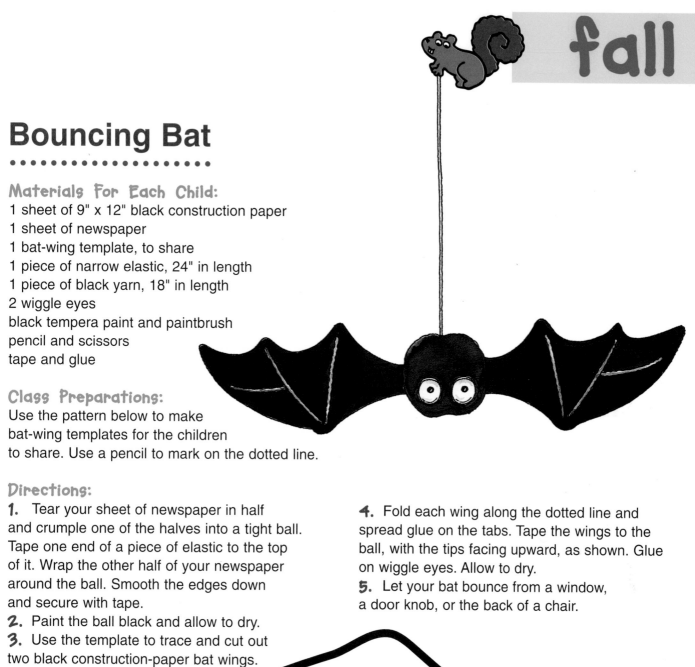

Bouncing Bat

. . . .

Materials For Each Child:
1 sheet of 9" x 12" black construction paper
1 sheet of newspaper
1 bat-wing template, to share
1 piece of narrow elastic, 24" in length
1 piece of black yarn, 18" in length
2 wiggle eyes
black tempera paint and paintbrush
pencil and scissors
tape and glue

Class Preparations:
Use the pattern below to make
bat-wing templates for the children
to share. Use a pencil to mark on the dotted line.

Directions:
1. Tear your sheet of newspaper in half and crumple one of the halves into a tight ball. Tape one end of a piece of elastic to the top of it. Wrap the other half of your newspaper around the ball. Smooth the edges down and secure with tape.
2. Paint the ball black and allow to dry.
3. Use the template to trace and cut out two black construction-paper bat wings. Mark on the dotted line. Cut the black yarn into six pieces and glue on the wings to look like veins, as shown. ⊕

4. Fold each wing along the dotted line and spread glue on the tabs. Tape the wings to the ball, with the tips facing upward, as shown. Glue on wiggle eyes. Allow to dry.
5. Let your bat bounce from a window, a door knob, or the back of a chair.

fold

Jack-O'-Lantern

. . . .

Materials For Each Child:
1 sheet of 9" x 12" black construction paper
1 glass jar
1 night light or glowstick
pencil, scissors, and tape

Directions:
1. Cut a strip of black construction paper to fit around the jar.
2. Draw simple jack-o'-lantern features on the paper. Cut out the features (see Practical Tips, page 4).

3. Wrap the paper around your jar. Tape the ends together to secure.
4. Place a night light or glowstick inside the jar. Turn out the lights and watch the spooky glow! Ⓣ

Halloween Banner

. . . .

Materials For Each Child:
1 sheet of 9" x 12" black construction paper
1 sheet of 9" x 12" colored construction paper
1 pumpkin, 1 cat, and 1 broom template,
   to share
colored construction-paper scraps
pencil, scissors, and glue

Class Preparations:
For this group activity, use the patterns on the opposite page to make templates for the children to share. Have tape ready.

Directions:
1. Use the templates to trace and cut out a few Halloween shapes from black construction paper.
2. Glue the shapes on a sheet of colored construction paper.
3. Cut one set of features for the jack-o'-lantern and two eyes for each cat from scraps of colored construction paper. Glue them in place.
4. Tape all the different-colored sheets of paper together to make a classroom banner. Ⓣ

fall

Use with Halloween Banner
on page 26.

27

Jack-O'-Lantern Parade

Materials For Each Child:
1 square of black construction paper, 6" x 6"
1 square of orange cellophane, 6" x 6"
1 pumpkin template, to share
pencil, scissors, and glue

Class Preparations:
For this group activity, use the pattern on the opposite page to make pumpkin templates for the children to share. Have tape and a length of clothesline ready.

Directions:
1. Use the template to trace and cut out a black construction-paper pumpkin.

2. Draw on a simple jack-o'-lantern face. Cut out the features (see Practical Tips, page 4).
3. Glue orange cellophane to the back of the jack-o'-lantern. Allow to dry; then trim the excess.
4. Tape the jack-o'-lanterns on a clothesline or in a line across a window to make a spooky pumpkin parade. Ⓣ

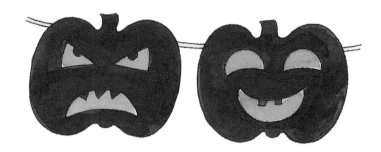

Pumpkin Patch

Materials For Each Child:
1 sheet of 9" x 12" dark blue construction paper
1 square of orange construction paper, 6" x 6"
1/4 sheet of 9" x 12" green construction paper
1 piece of green yarn, 18" in length
pumpkin, leaf, and star templates, to share
aluminum-foil scraps
black markers
pencil, scissors, and glue

Class Preparations:
For this group activity, use the patterns on the opposite page to make pumpkin, leaf, and star templates for the children to share. Have tape ready.

Directions:
1. Use the templates to trace and cut out an orange pumpkin and a green leaf.
2. Glue the pumpkin to the middle of the dark blue paper. Use a marker to draw red ridges on the pumpkin.

3. Glue yarn across the paper, over the pumpkin stalk, looping it to make a vine. Leave 2" free at each end. Glue the leaf on the vine.
4. Use the star template to trace and cut out several aluminum-foil stars. Glue these on the picture.
5. Tape the pictures together in a line to make a pumpkin patch. Tie the free ends of yarn together to make one long vine. Ⓣ

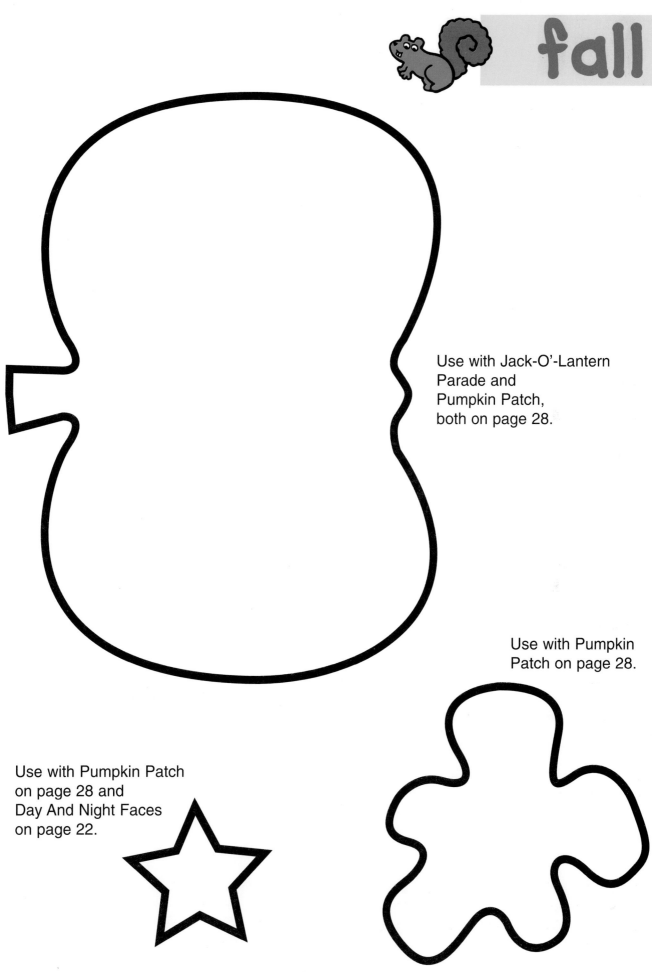

fall

Use with Jack-O'-Lantern
Parade and
Pumpkin Patch,
both on page 28.

Use with Pumpkin
Patch on page 28.

Use with Pumpkin Patch
on page 28 and
Day And Night Faces
on page 22.

Trick-Or-Treat Bucket

Materials For Each Child:
1 sheet of 9" x 12" black construction paper
1 clean yogurt container
1 bat template, to share
strips of orange, yellow, and red cellophane,
    about 4" in length
several wrapped candies
pencil and ruler
scissors, tape, and glue

Class Preparations:
Use the pattern below to make bat templates for
the children to share. Cut strips of cellophane,
about 4" in length.

Directions:
1. Use a pencil and ruler to draw and cut a
black construction-paper strip, 9" long and
$1/2$" wide. Tape the strip to the container to
make a handle. Ⓗ
2. Cut a piece of black construction paper to
fit around the container. Glue in place.
3. Cut the ends of the cellophane strips to
look like flames; then glue them around the
bottom of the container.
4. Use the template to trace and cut three
black construction-paper bats.
5. Place the bats and several candies inside
your trick-or-treat bucket. Ask your friends to
close their eyes and pick out the first thing
they touch in the bucket. Will it be a candy
treat or a trick bat?

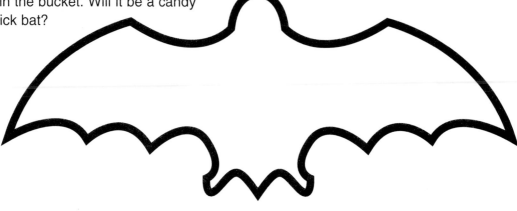

Terrific turkey ideas will add plenty of extra zip to your Thanksgiving celebrations!

Thanksgiving Turkey Mask

Materials For Each Child:
1 sheet of 9" x 12" brown construction paper
1 paper plate, 7" in diameter
1 piece of elastic, 10" in length
orange tempera paint and paintbrush
sharp pencil
ruler, scissors, and glue

Directions:

1. Fold the paper plate in half and cut out a wedge, as shown (A). Open out the triangular wedge and paint it orange to make a beak.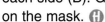

2. Use a pencil to make a hole in each side of the plate (see Practical Tips, page 4). Thread elastic through and tie in a knot at the back. Then make two large eyeholes near the center of the plate. (H)

3. Cut a sheet of brown paper into short strips, 1" wide. Cut a fringe along one side of each strip; then glue around the plate in circular layers to look like feathers. (H)

4. Make a small cut in the top of the beak and fold back the paper on each side (B). Glue the flaps on the mask. (H)

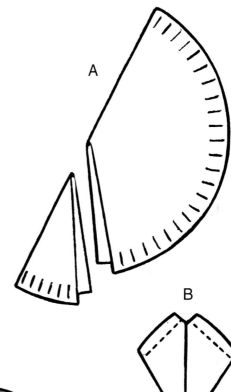

A

B

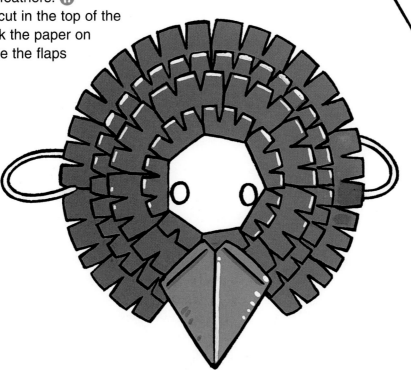

Wobbling Turkey

Materials For Each Child:
1 sheet of 9" x 12" light brown
   construction paper, with turkey
   head outline
1 large paper cup
1 yellow pipe cleaner, cut in halves
2 pieces of modeling clay, each about
   the size of a ping-pong ball
colored crayons
pencil, scissors, tape, and glue

Class Preparations:
For each child, duplicate the head pattern below
on a sheet of 9" x 12" light brown construction
paper. Cut pipe cleaners into halves and use a
craft knife to cut a 1" slit in the base of each cup.

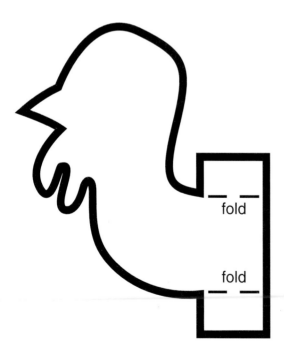

fold

fold

Directions:
1. Cut out the turkey head. Color a wattle, beak,
and eye on each side. Fold in the flaps on each
side of the turkey's neck and insert through the
slit in the cup. Open out the flaps inside the cup
to hold the head in place. (H)
2. Make 2" cuts all around the top of the cup.
Curl each piece tightly around a pencil to make
the turkey's tail.
3. Use a pencil to make two holes in the side
of the cup, close to each other, for feet (see
Practical Tips, page 4). Push half a pipe cleaner
through each hole; then bend back the portion
inside the cup and tape to secure. (H)
4. Accordion-fold the remaining brown paper.
Draw feathers on the top section and cut through
all the layers to make several feathers at once.
Snip around the edges of each feather. Glue the
feathers on the turkey's body. Allow to dry.
5. Mold each piece of modeling clay to look like
a turkey's foot. Push the pipe-cleaner legs into
the clay feet to stand up your turkey. Gently push
the turkey's body to make it wobble!

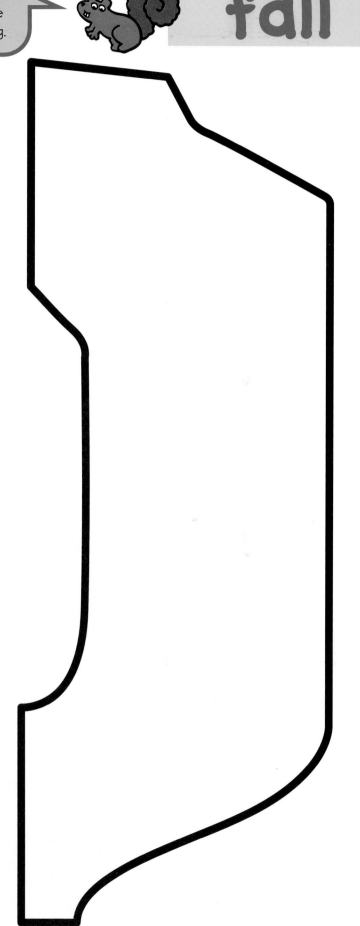

Mayflower

Materials For Each Child:
1 sheet of 9" x 12" blue construction paper
$\frac{1}{2}$ sheet of 9" x 12" brown construction paper
1 ship-hull template, to share
1 small, branched twig
1 small piece of thin white fabric
pretzel sticks
white tempera paint and paintbrush
pencil, scissors, and glue

Class Preparations:
Use the pattern on the right to make ship-hull templates for the children to share. Have the children collect small branched twigs. Cut sheets of brown construction paper into halves.

Directions:
1. Paint white waves on a sheet of blue construction paper to make a sea background.
2. Trace the ship-hull template onto brown construction paper and cut out.
3. Glue the hull on the bottom of the painted seascape.
4. Glue pretzels on the hull to resemble wooden planks.
5. Place the twig above the hull. Spread glue on the white fabric and stick down over the twig, on the blue paper, for a mast and sail.

33

Snail Place Cards

. . . .

Materials For Each Child:

½ sheet of 9" x 12" light brown
  construction paper
1 snail template, to share
8 pieces of different-colored yarn, 12" in length
2 pieces of white string or pipe cleaner,
  1" in length
black marker, pencil, scissors, and glue

Class Preparations:

Use the pattern on the right to make snail
templates for the children to share. Cut a
piece of 9" x 6" brown construction paper
for each child.

Directions:

1. Fold the brown construction paper in half.
Line up the top of the snail template with the
fold. Trace around the shape; then cut it out,
but do not cut along the fold.

2. Spread glue on one side of the snail where
the shell belongs. Wind a piece of yarn around
the shell in a spiral, beginning at the edge and
working inwards. When the yarn runs out,
continue with another piece in a different
color. Allow to dry.

3. Repeat on the other side of the snail.

4. Glue a short piece of
string or pipe cleaner on
each side of the snail's
head for antennae. Use a
marker to draw an eye and
a mouth on each side.

5. Write your name on
each side at the bottom
of the card. Use a
marker to draw a
brick wall around
your name.

fold

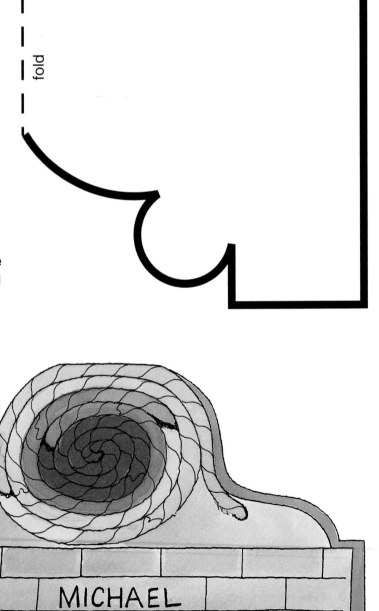

winter

Discuss with the class how some animals hibernate throughout the winter months.

Who's Hibernating?

Materials For Each Child:
½ sheet of 9" x 12" black construction paper
½ sheet of 9" x 12" white drawing paper
2 wiggle eyes
pencil
scissors
glue

Class Preparations:
For each child, cut a 9" x 6" piece of black construction paper and a 9" x 6" piece of white drawing paper.

Directions:
1. Mark out the shape of a cave on the black construction paper.
2. Cut a strip, about 9" long, of jagged icicles from white drawing paper and glue it along the top of the cave.
3. Tear the rest of the white paper into squares about 1" x 1". Glue them all around the cave to cover the rest of the paper. Overlap the pieces so that no black paper shows.
4. Glue the wiggle eyes in the center of the cave. Whooo's there?

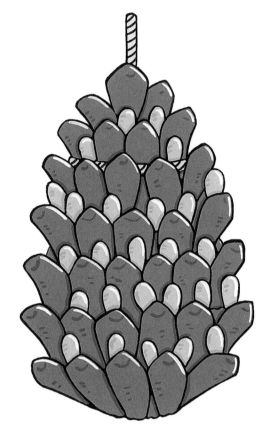

Pine Cone Bird Feeder

Materials For Each Child:
1 pine cone
1 piece of string, 20" in length
shelled sunflower seeds
suet

Class Preparations:
Have your class collect pine cones; then leave the cones in a warm place until they are dry and open.

Directions:
1. Tie string around the top of the pine cone.
2. Use your fingers to push suet into the cone.
3. Push sunflower seeds into the suet.
4. Hang the cone from a branch outdoors on a fine day and watch the birds feed. Ⓗ

Robin In The Snow

· ·

Materials For Each Child:
1 sheet of 9" x 12" white
   construction paper
1 robin template, to share
5 or 6 cotton balls
brown and red tissue paper
yellow construction-paper scrap
yellow and black markers
pencil, scissors, and glue

Class Preparations:
Use the pattern below to make robin
templates for the children to share.

Directions:
1. Fold the sheet of construction
paper in half widthwise to make a card.
2. Use the template to trace a robin
outline on the card. Draw a pencil line
to mark out the robin's breast.
3. Tear the tissue paper into small pieces;
then spread glue on the robin and stick
on the pieces, overlapping them as you go.
Use red for the robin's breast and brown
for the rest of the body.
4. Cut a triangle for the beak from yellow
construction paper; then glue on the robin's
head. Use markers to add legs and an eye.
5. Give your robin a snowy setting
by gluing cotton balls on
the bottom of the card.

Mega Bird Feeder

Materials For Each Child:
2 plastic cups
2 clean, wooden skewers
1 piece of plastic or nylon string, 18" in length
birdseed
glue and waterproof tape

Class Preparations:
For each child, use a sharp pencil or scissors to make a small hole in the base of each cup. Make several holes in the sides of one of the cups, big enough to pull seeds through. Push two skewers through the lower part of this cup to make a cross.

Directions:
1. Tie a knot at one end of the string. Thread it through the hole in the bottom of the cup holding the skewers, so that the knot is on the outside. (H)
2. Turn the other cup upside-down and thread the string through it, to make the top of the feeder.
3. Pour birdseed and nuts into the bottom cup, keeping the top cup out of the way.
4. Spread glue around the rim of the bottom cup, then press the other cup's rim onto it. Secure with tape. (H)
5. Hang the feeder from a branch. (H)

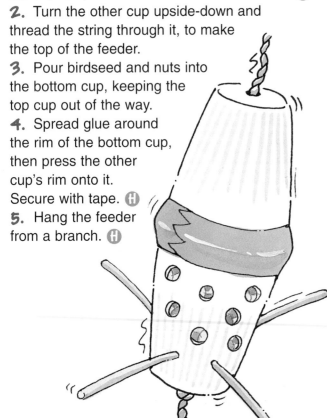

Silvery Scene

Materials For Each Child:
1 piece of heavy-duty aluminum foil, about 5" x 8"
1/2 sheet of 9" x 12" dark blue construction paper
silver marker and soft pencil
black tempera paint and paintbrush
damp paper towels
several sheets of newspaper
glue

Class Preparations:
For each child, cut a 9" x 6" piece of construction paper. Dampen a supply of paper towels.

Directions:
1. Fold several sheets of newspaper to make a padded work surface. Place the foil on the newspaper.
2. Draw a design on the foil with the pencil, pressing gently.
3. Brush black paint over the foil, then dab the foil gently with a paper towel to remove excess paint. Allow to dry for about an hour.
4. Glue the picture to the blue construction paper; then use a silver marker to decorate the blue background with tiny dots.

Tree Silhouette

Materials For Each Child:
1 black tagboard frame, 9" x 12"
1/2 sheet of 9" x 12" black construction paper
1/2 sheet of 12" x 18" light blue tissue paper
1 piece of waxed paper, 9" x 12"
scissors and glue

Class Preparations:
For each child, cut a rectangle from the center of a sheet of 9" x 12" black tagboard, to leave a frame, 1" wide. Also, cut a piece of 9" x 12" of light blue tissue paper.

Directions:
1. Spread glue on one side of the frame, then press onto a sheet of tissue paper. Glue the same side of the frame again and press onto waxed paper. Allow to dry; then trim the tissue and waxed paper to the edge of the frame.
2. Cut a tree trunk shape from black paper; then cut lots of thin strips for branches. Glue the trunk and branches on the tissue paper. Allow to dry.
3. Display the picture on a window or windowsill so that light shines through.

Falling Snowflakes

Materials For Each Child:
1 sheet of 9" x 12" blue construction paper
1/4 sheet of 9" x 12" white drawing paper
1/6 sheet of 12" x 18" white tissue paper
green tempera paint and paintbrush
sharp pencil
glitter and glue

Directions:
1. Tear white drawing paper into small pieces. Glue the pieces along the bottom of the blue paper to resemble snow on the ground.
2. Paint several green trees above the snow.
3. Make 15–20 holes in the paper above the trees with a sharp pencil (see Practical Tips, page 4).
4. Tear white tissue paper into 1" squares. Push the paper through the holes, from front to back, leaving the ends poking through.
5. Dab glue on the snowy areas; then sprinkle on glitter.

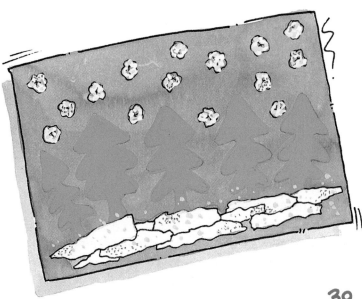

These attractive Christmas projects are simple to make and give stunning results. Try them out!

Reindeer Antlers

Materials For Each Child:
2 sheets of 9" x 12" tagboard
1 strip of construction paper, 1" x 18"
stapler to share
brown or red tempera paint
paintbrush, ruler, and scissors

Class Preparations:
Organize the children to work in pairs, taking turns to paint each other's hands.

Directions:
1. Have a friend paint the palm of your hand. Spread your fingers out, then place your hand firmly on a sheet of tagboard. Press on the back of one hand with your other hand. Lift off carefully and allow to dry. Wash your hand.
2. Repeat with your other hand.
3. Cut around the handprints. Leave a wide border and a wide tab about 2" long at the bottom of each print.
4. Staple the tab of each print to the construction-paper strip. 🄗
5. Wrap the strip around your head; then cut the ends and staple to make a headband. 🄗

Wax-Resist Snowman

Materials For Each Child:
½ sheet of 9" x 12" white construction paper
1 white candle
3 buttons
2 short pieces of white pipe cleaner
1 short piece of black pipe cleaner
2 wiggle eyes
black and orange construction-paper scraps
dark blue tempera paint and paintbrush
pencil, scissors, and glue

Class Preparations:
For each child, cut a 9" x 6" piece of white construction paper. Cut white and black pipe cleaners into short lengths.

Directions:
1. Use a pencil to draw on white paper the outline of a snowman standing on snow.
2. Rub the candle like a crayon over the snowman and snow. Add dots of snow to the sky.
3. Paint all over with blue paint. Allow to dry.
4. Draw and cut out a nose from orange paper and a hat from black paper. Glue them on the snowman's head.
5. Finally, glue on a black pipe-cleaner mouth, wiggle eyes, buttons, and white pipe-cleaner arms.

Snowman Chain

Materials For Each Child:
1/2 sheet of 12" x 18" white construction paper
1 snowman template, to share
crayons
scissors
ruler and pencil

Class Preparations:
For each child, cut a 6" x 18" strip of white construction paper. Use the pattern below to make snowman templates for the children to share.

Directions:
1. Use a ruler and pencil to divide the strip of paper into six sections, each 3" wide. 🄷
2. Accordion-fold the paper along the lines.
3. Use the template to trace a snowman on the top section of the folded paper.
4. Cut around the shape, but don't cut around the ends of each arm.
5. Unfold the paper and decorate your snowmen with crayons.
6. Line up all the snowmen to create a wintery bulletin-board trim. 🅣

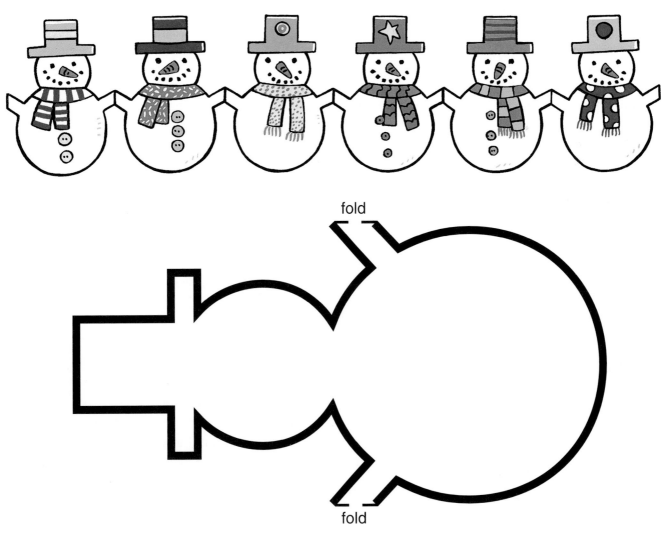

fold

fold

Wintery Skyline Card

Materials For Each Child:
½ sheet of 12" x 18" white construction paper
⅙ sheet of 12" x 18" blue tissue paper
white and yellow construction-paper scraps
black, gray, and white tempera paints
paintbrushes
a Q-Tip®
pencil, scissors, glitter, and glue

Class Preparations:
For each child, cut a 6" x 18" piece of
construction paper. Accordion-fold the paper into
three sections (A). Provide children with pictures
of skylines in cities, towns, or villages.

Directions:
1. Draw a skyline on the front section of the
card, on the lower half of the paper. Cut off the
part above the line (B).
2. Draw a skyline on the middle section, higher
than the first skyline, and cut this out, too (C).
3. Paint the middle section black and the front
section gray. Allow to dry.
4. Cut out tiny squares and rectangles from
white and yellow construction paper. Glue them
to the buildings to make windows.
5. Tear strips of blue tissue paper and glue all
over the back section. Allow to dry.
6. Paint on tiny white dots for snow with a Q-Tip®
and paint narrow white lines along the rooftops
with a paintbrush. Paint on stars and a moon.
When dry, spread glue on the stars and moon
and sprinkle on glitter.

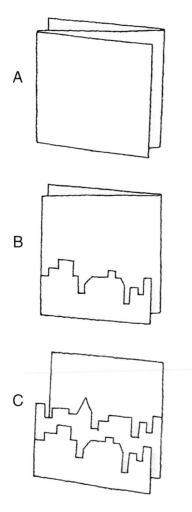

Reindeer Magnet

Materials For Each Child:
1 tagboard square, 6" x 6"
1 reindeer template
1 square of gift wrap, 6" x 6", with a small pattern
1 magnet or strip of self-adhesive magnetic tape
glue and paintbrush
pencil and black marker

Class Preparations:
Use the pattern below to make a reindeer template for each child.

Directions:
1. Glue gift wrap to a square of tagboard.
2. Turn over the tagboard so that the gift wrap faces down, and use the template to trace a reindeer shape on the tagboard. Cut out the reindeer.
3. Use a black marker to add eyes to the patterned side of the reindeer.
4. Brush glue all over the gift wrap to make it shine. Allow to dry.
5. Glue a magnet to the back or stick on magnetic tape.

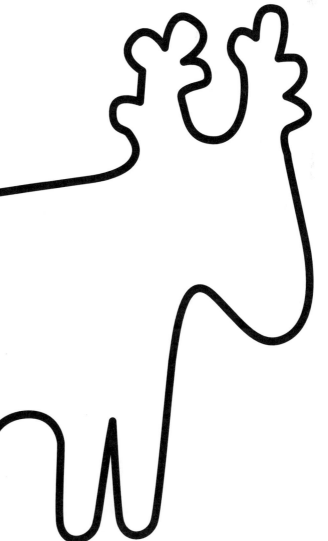

Make your classroom special with inexpensive, handmade decorations. Here are lots of bright ideas!

Christmas Treat Bag

Materials For Each Child:
1 brown lunch bag
1 narrow ribbon or piece of yarn, 25" in length
white tempera paint and paintbrush
hole puncher to share
small gifts or candies
black marker, glitter, and glue

Directions:

1. Use a hole puncher to punch a row of holes around the top of the bag, about ¹/₂" from the bag's edge. (H)

2. Paint on snowy ground, a snowman's head and body, and snowflakes falling. Allow to dry.

3. Use a marker to add a face, hat, arms, and buttons.

4. Spread glue on the snowy ground and sprinkle on glitter. Allow to dry.

5. Fill the bag with little gifts, such as candies.

6. Thread a ribbon or yarn through the holes and pull gently to close the bag. Then tie the ends in a bow.

Glitter-Ball Tree Decorations

Materials For Each Child:
1 piece of string, 6" long
newspaper
flour-and-water paste
scraps of colored paper, gift wrap, or magazines
tempera paint and paintbrush
masking tape
glitter and glue

Class Preparations:
Make up flour-and-water paste for the class (see page 5).

Directions:

1. Crumple a sheet of newspaper into a ball about the size of a tennis ball.

2. Wrap tape around the ball to keep it in shape. Tape on a loop of string. (H)

3. Tear more newspaper into strips. Spread paste on each strip and stick on the ball. Overlap the strips until the ball is covered. Allow to dry.

4. Decorate the ball either by painting it or by gluing on scraps of torn paper. Dot with glue and sprinkle on glitter.

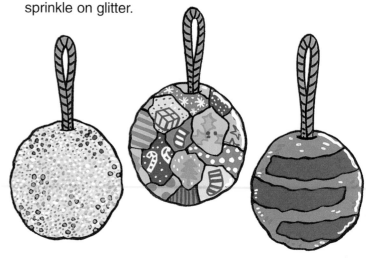

Sparkly Shapes

Materials For Each Child:

1/3 sheet of 9" x 12" white construction paper,
  with star, diamond, and triangle outlines
3 ribbons or pieces of yarn, each 6" in length
colored paper and aluminum-foil scraps
scissors, tape, glitter, and glue

Class Preparations:

For each child, duplicate the patterns on the
right on one third of a sheet of 9" x 12" white
construction paper.

Directions:

1. Cut out the three shapes.
2. Use tape to attach a loop of ribbon
to the top of each shape.
3. Glue paper scraps and foil all over
the shapes, front and back, making
sure you cover up the tape.
Trim the uneven edges.
4. Spread glue around the edge
of each shape and sprinkle
on glitter. Allow to dry.
5. Hang the shapes
on a Christmas tree.

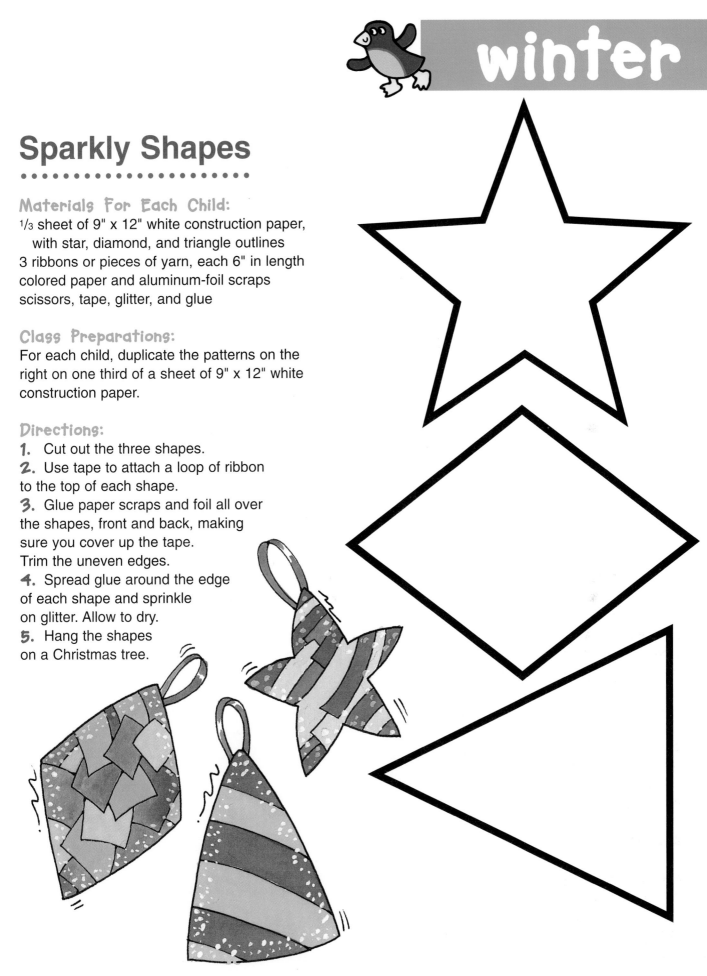

45

Holiday Box

· · · · · · · · · · · · · · · · · · · ·

Materials For Each Child:
1 sheet of 9" x 12" green construction paper
1 box template
a length of ribbon or yarn
colored paper scraps and glitter
hole puncher to share
tempera paints and paintbrushes
pencil and ruler
scissors and glue

Class Preparations:
Use the pattern on the opposite page to make a box template for each child. Mark on the dotted line above the flap.

Directions:
1. Use a ruler and pencil to divide the sheet of green paper into four sections, each 3" wide. ⑪
2. Accordion-fold the paper along the lines; then trace around the template on the top section.
3. Cut out the shape, but do not cut along the folds (A). Use a hole puncher to punch a hole in the top. Open the paper out. ⑪
4. Using the template as a guide, fold the flap at the bottom of each section of paper. Cut off the flap on the last section (B).
5. Decorate the first three sections with paints or paper scraps. Add glitter and allow to dry.
6. Spread glue over the fourth section and stick it inside the first, to make a three-sided box. ⑪
7. Glue together the flaps to make the base. ⑪
8. Thread a piece of ribbon or yarn through the punched holes and tie the ends to add a finishing touch. ⑪

A

B

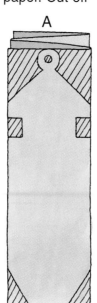

Use with Holiday Box on page 46.

winter

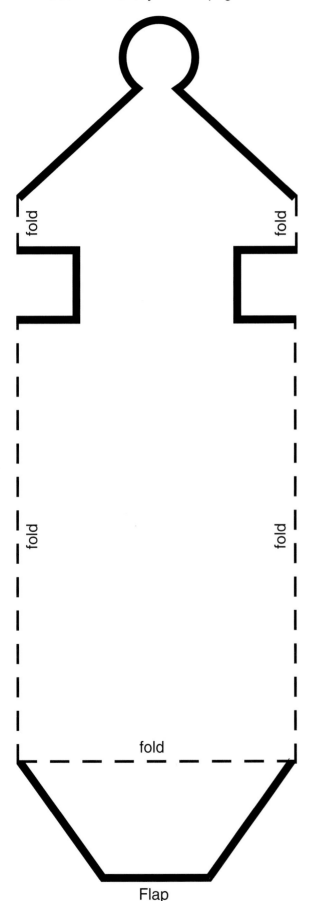

fold

fold

fold

fold

fold

Flap

Printed Place Mats

● ●

Materials For Each Child:
4 sheets of 9" x 12" white construction paper
½ potato
red, green, and gold tempera paints
  in shallow dishes
paintbrush and scissors

Class Preparations:
Cut potatoes in half and draw a star on each
cut surface. (You could use the star pattern on
page 29.) Use a craft knife to cut away the potato
from around the star, leaving a raised shape.

Directions:
1. Dip the potato star into red or green paint.
Press it onto a sheet of construction paper, about
2" from the edge. Continue printing around the
paper to make a border. Remember to wash the
potato each time you change color. Allow to dry.
2. Repeat to make three more mats.
3. Paint a gold square around the center
of each mat, as shown.
4. When dry, stack the mats neatly. Cut a fringe,
1" long, around the edges of the mats, cutting
through all four layers at the same time.

Curly Bearded Santa

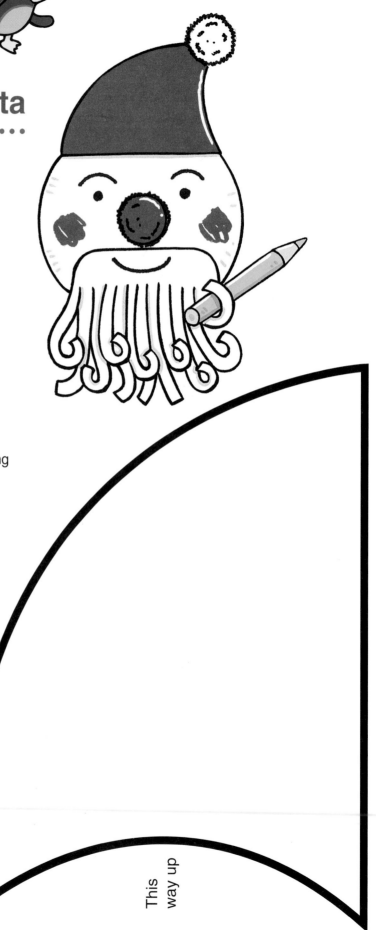

Materials For Each Child:
1/2 sheet of 9" x 12" red construction paper
1 hat template, to share
1 large red pompom
1 large white pompom
1 square of white drawing paper, 6" x 6"
1 paper plate, 7" in diameter
red and black markers
pencil and ruler
scissors and glue

Class Preparations:
Use the pattern below to make hat templates for the children to share.

Directions:
1. First, make Santa's beard. Start by rounding the corners of the drawing paper; then cut slits along the bottom, about 1/2" apart and to about 1" from the top.

2. Curl each paper strip by pressing the edge of a pencil firmly along it.

3. Glue the curly beard about 2" from the bottom edge of the plate.

4. Use the template to trace a hat on red paper. Cut it out and glue on the plate, as shown. Glue a white pompom on the end of the hat.

5. Glue a red pompom on the plate for Santa's nose; then use markers to add eyes, eyebrows, cheeks, and a smiling mouth.

This way up

48

Stained-Glass Star

Materials For Each Child:
2 star-shaped black construction-paper frames
1 white tissue-paper square, 6" x 6"
colored tissue-paper scraps
thread and tape
scissors and glue

Class Preparations:
Use the pattern below to cut two stars for
each child from black construction paper.
Cut out the center of each star with
a craft knife to leave a frame.

Directions:
1. Spread glue over one of the frames
and lay on the white tissue paper.
2. Glue on overlapping scraps of
colored tissue paper to cover the
white tissue paper. Allow to dry.
3. Carefully trim any paper
that extends beyond
the edges of the star.

4. Tape a loop of thread
to one of the star points.
5. Spread glue over
the second star frame.
6. Press onto the first frame,
making sure the edges of
both frames line up.

49

Christmas Garland

Materials For Each Child:
1 sheet of 9" x 12" colored construction paper,
  cut in half
1 piece of yarn, 30" in length
sequins and colored markers
scissors, pencil, and glue

Class Preparations:
For each child, cut a sheet of construction
paper into two strips, each 4½" x 12".

Directions:
1. Fold each strip of paper in half lengthwise.
2. Draw a simple shape, such as one of those
shown below, several times along the fold.
3. Cut out the shapes. Do not cut along the fold.
4. Open out each shape and decorate
one side with sequins and markers.
5. Spread glue on the inside
of the fold and attach the shapes
at intervals along
a length of yarn.

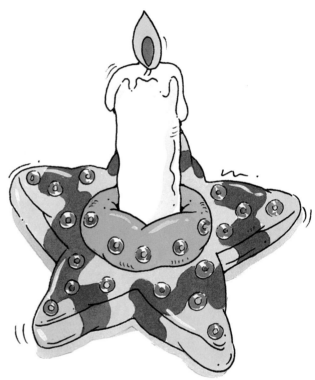

Star Of Wonder
Candle Holder

Materials For Each Child:
self-hardening modeling clay,
  about the size of a baseball
a candle
a rolling pin to share
a large star-shaped cookie cutter, to share
tempera paints and paintbrushes
sequins and glue

Directions:
1. Use a rolling pin to roll out the modeling
clay to a depth of about ¾". Cut out a star
shape with a cookie cutter.
2. Use the leftover clay to mold a ping-pong
sized ball. Flatten the ball slightly and press
in the candle to make a hollow. Remove the
candle and allow the clay pieces to harden.
3. Glue the flattened ball in the center
of the star.
4. Decorate your candle holder with paint.
5. When dry, glue on sequins.

Woven Tree Decoration

Materials For Each Child:

8 pieces of colored construction paper,
 each 4" x ½"
1 narrow ribbon, 6" in length
a selection of narrow colored construction-paper
 strips, all at least 5" in length
ruler, pencil, glue, and scissors

Class Preparations:

For each child, cut eight strips of construction
paper, each measuring 4" x ½". These will
make two frames.

Directions:

1. Glue four pieces of construction paper
together at the corners to make a square frame.
Repeat with the other four pieces to make a
second frame. ⊞

2. Spread glue along the top edge of one frame.
Lay several narrow paper strips along the glued
edge so that they extend below the bottom of the
frame. Leave a small gap between each strip.
Allow to dry. ⊞

3. Glue one end of a paper strip to the top of the
left-hand edge of the frame. Weave it alternately
over and under the strips attached in step 2, until
you reach the right-hand edge of the frame.
Glue the end. ⊞

4. Repeat step 3 with another strip, and
then another, working your way down
the frame until you reach the bottom (A).

5. Glue a loop of ribbon to one corner of
the frame, as shown (B). Glue the empty
frame on top of the woven frame. Trim
the ragged edges.

B

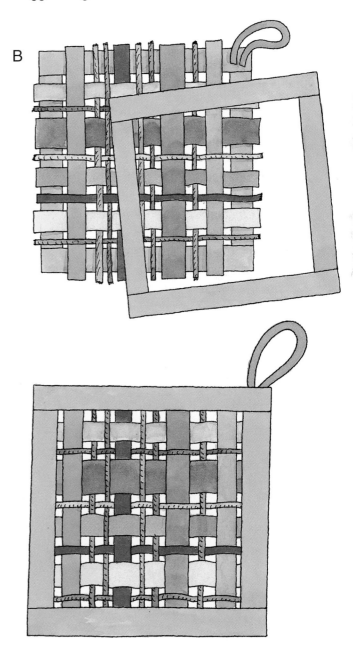

A

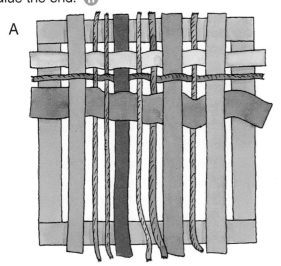

Christmas Bell

• •

Materials For Each Child:
1 paper cup
1 piece of string, 10" in length
1 jingle bell
newspaper
flour-and-water paste
tempera paints
paintbrushes
pencil

Class Preparations:
Make up a flour-and-water paste (see page 5).

Directions:
1. Tear newspaper into strips. Paste four layers all over the outside of the cup. Allow to dry.
2. Use a pencil to make a hole in the bottom of the cup (see Practical Tips, page 4).
3. Paint a colorful pattern on the cup and allow to dry.
4. Tie a jingle bell to one end of the string. ⊕
5. Tie a double knot in the string, about 5" from the bell. Thread the end of the string through the hole in the cup from the inside. ⊕
6. Tie a loop in the end of the string for hanging the bell. ⊕

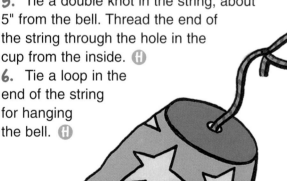

Trotting Reindeer

• •

Materials For Each Child:
1 sheet of 9" x 12" tan-colored tagboard, with outlines of a reindeer's head, body, and legs
2 wiggle eyes
4 brass fasteners
white tissue-paper scraps
black and red markers, scissors, and glue

Class Preparations:
For each child, duplicate the patterns on the opposite page on tan-colored tagboard.

Directions:
1. Cut out the reindeer's body, head, and four legs. Fold the body in half along the dotted line.
2. Crumple small pieces of white tissue paper into balls. Glue them on the reindeer's body.
3. Color the reindeer's hoofs black and color its nose red. Glue on wiggle eyes.
4. Attach each leg by pushing a brass fastener through the leg and the body, where marked. ⊕
5. Glue the head to the body.

Use with Trotting Reindeer on page 52.

Body

fold

Legs

Head

53

These gift-wrapping ideas will teach your students new art techniques and add zest to all their Christmas gifts!

Butterfly Pin

Materials For Each Child:
1 piece of felt, 4" x 4½"
a wooden clothespin
colored sequins
colored markers
a Q-Tip®
scissors and glue

Directions:

1. Fold the felt in half. Draw a butterfly's wing next to the fold, as shown (A).
2. Cut around the shape but do not cut along the fold.
3. Use a Q-Tip® to dot glue on the felt; then stick on sequins. Keep the two wing designs symmetrical.
4. To make the butterfly's body, draw stripes on the clothespin and eyes at the top.
5. Glue the back of the felt to the clothespin.
6. Why not use your butterfly pin to decorate a tree or to clip Christmas cards on a card line?

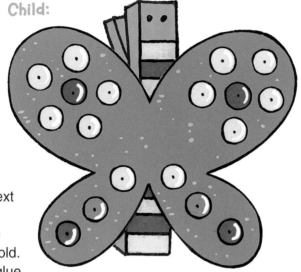

A

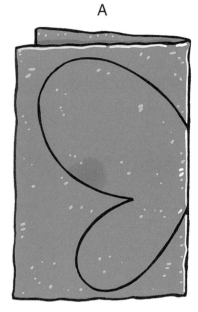

Wax-Resist Gift Wrap

Materials For Each Child:
2 sheets of 9" x 12" white construction paper
a candle
tempera paints and paintbrushes
pencil

Directions:

1. Draw a design lightly in pencil on each sheet of construction paper.
2. Draw over the pencil lines with the end of a candle.
3. Use a paintbrush to cover the whole sheet of paper with paint. You could use several colors, or just one.

Golden Gift Tags

Materials For Each Child:
1/3 sheet of 9" x 12" tagboard
2 ribbons, 6" in length
2 pieces of string, 6" in length
gold spray paint
gold glitter
hole puncher, to share
scissors, glue and paintbrush

Class Preparations:
For each child, cut two pieces
of 4" x 4 1/2 " tagboard.

Directions:

1. Cut two tagboard pieces into different
gift tag shapes, such as a circle, a triangle,
or a diamond.

2. Brush glue all over each tag, then lay on
a piece of string to make a design. Allow to dry.

3. Spray gold paint all over the top of each tag. ⊤

4. Allow to dry; then glue on gold glitter.

5. Punch a hole in each tag and thread a
ribbon through. Tie ends of the ribbon together. ⊕

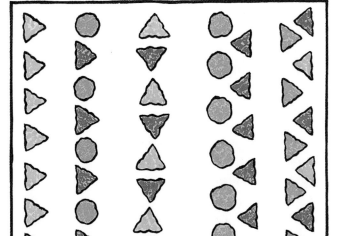

Sponged Gift Wrap

Materials For Each Child:
1 large sheet of bulletin-board paper
1 household sponge, no more than 1" thick
different-colored tempera paints in saucers
black fine-tip marker
scissors

Directions:

1. Use a marker to draw two or three shapes,
such as a triangle and a circle, on the surface
of the sponge. Cut out the shapes.

2. Dip each sponge in a different color of paint.

3. Dab each sponge onto paper lots of times
to make a repeated pattern.

Festive Tree Card

Materials For Each Child:
1 sheet of 9" x 12" white construction paper
½ sheet of 9" x 12" green construction paper
1 tree, 1 trunk, and 1 bucket template, to share
1 star sticker
red and brown construction-paper scraps
rickrack, sequins, and glitter
scraps of gift wrap
red marker, pencil, scissors, and glue

Class Preparations:
Use the patterns on the opposite page to make templates for the children to share. Cut a 9" x 6" piece of green construction paper for each child.

Directions:
1. Use the templates to trace and cut out a tree from green paper, a trunk from brown paper, and a bucket shape from red paper.

2. Fold the white construction paper in half to make a card. Glue on the bucket, the trunk, and the tree.
3. Glue rickrack across the tree as garlands; then glue on sequins. Dab glue on the edges of the tree and sprinkle on glitter.
4. Cut out pieces of gift wrap and glue them around the base of the tree, for gifts. Add the star sticker to the top of the tree.

Glass Candle Holder

Materials For Each Child:
1 glass jar
1 night light
star stickers
indelible markers
newspaper and tape

Directions:
1. Use indelible markers to draw a design on your glass jar.
2. Position star stickers around the jar.
3. Place a night light inside.
4. To take the candle holder home, carefully wrap the jar in several sheets of newspaper and secure with tape. ⊕

Use with Festive Tree Card
on page 56.

Tree

Trunk

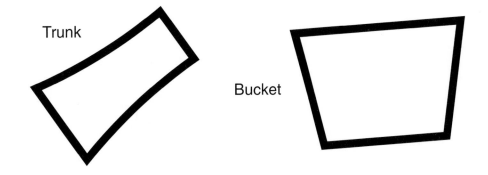

Bucket

winter

Use with Felt Stocking
on page 59.

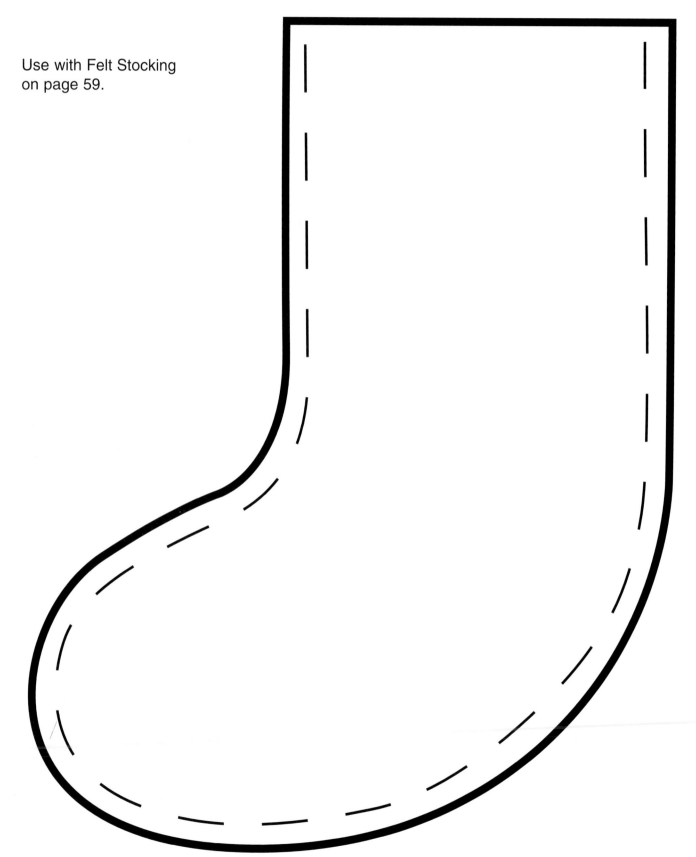

Felt Stocking

Materials For Each Child:
2 pieces of colored felt, 9" x 12"
1 stocking template
needle, pins, and thread
rickrack, pompoms, and jingle bells
marker, pencil, scissors, and glue

Class Preparations:
For each child, duplicate and cut out the pattern on the opposite page to make a template. Have a hot-glue gun ready.

Directions:
1. Use the template to trace and cut out two felt stockings.
2. Pin the stockings together and use a marker to draw the stitching lines on one side.
3. Thread the needle; then sew along the stitching lines, leaving the top open. **H**
4. Hot-glue bells to the top of the stocking. **T**
5. Glue rickrack and pom-poms to the stocking. Hang up your stocking and wait for Santa!

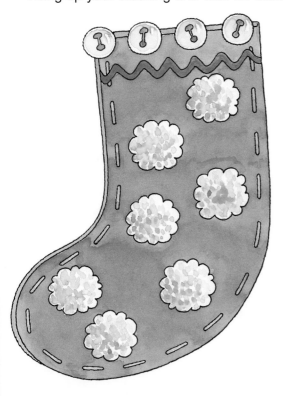

Penguin Party

Materials For Each Child:
1 sheet of 12" x 18" black construction paper
1 sheet of 9" x 12" white construction paper, with 5 penguin chest outlines
1/2 sheet of 9" x 12" orange construction paper
1 sheet of 12" x 18" blue bulletin-board paper
1 penguin template, pencil, scissors, and glue

Class Preparations:
Use the pattern on page 60 to make penguin body templates for the children to share. Duplicate the penguin chest pattern five times on white construction paper for each child.

Directions:
1. Use the template to trace the penguin body five times on black paper. Cut out the shapes.
2. Cut out the five white chest shapes.
3. Cut five triangles for beaks and ten feet from orange paper. Tear five tiny pieces of white paper to make eyes.
4. Turn some of the body shapes over to make the penguin face the opposite way. Glue a white chest on each penguin body; then glue on the beak, feet, and eyes.
5. Arrange the penguins on blue bulletin-board paper and glue in position.

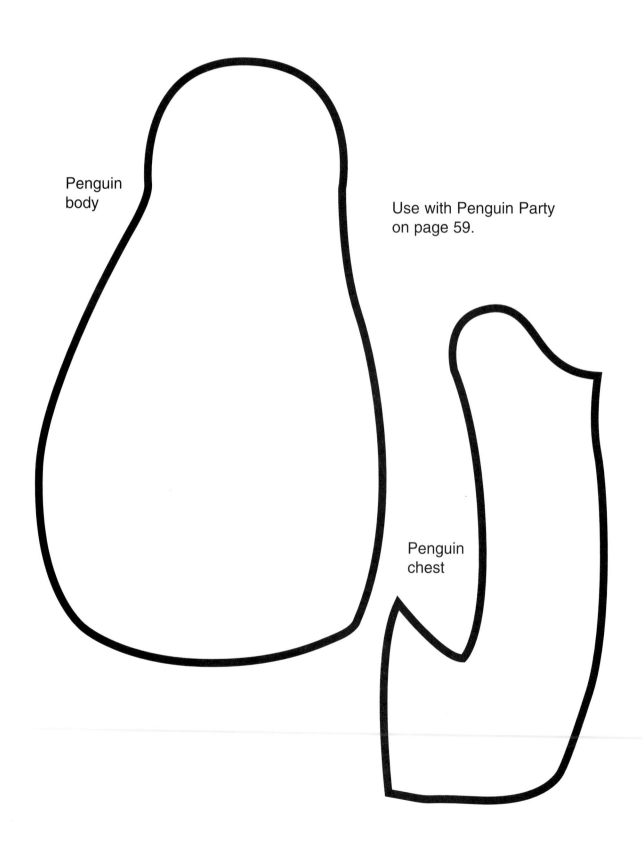

Penguin
body

Use with Penguin Party
on page 59.

Penguin
chest

Why not show your students pictures of polar lands? Then find out how people and animals live in icy regions.

Ducks On Ice

Materials For Each Child:
1 sheet of 12" x 18" light blue
  construction paper
1 sheet of 9" x 12" white
  construction paper, with 3
  duck outlines
1 piece of clear plastic wrap,
  about 12" x 18"
white tempera paint and paintbrush
double-sided tape
orange and black markers
scissors, glitter, and glue

Class Preparations:
Duplicate the pattern below three times on white construction paper for each child.

Directions:
1. Cut out an irregular pond shape from light blue paper. Add a few strokes of white paint and allow to dry.
2. Dab glue around the edges of the pond and sprinkle on glitter. Allow to dry.
3. Use double-sided tape to stick clear plastic wrap over the pond. Trim the edges of the wrap. Ⓗ
4. Cut out the three ducks. Color the feet and beak orange; then add a black eye and a wing outline.
5. Glue the ducks to the icy pond.

Polar Pals

• • • • • • • • • • • • • •

Materials For Each Child:
1 seal, 1 fish head, and 1 fish tail template,
  to share
1 square of light blue construction
  paper, 12" x 12"
dark gray construction paper scraps
white Styrofoam® scraps
silver paper scraps
dark blue tempera paint and paintbrush
black marker
pencil, scissors, and glue

Class Preparations:
Use the patterns below to provide seal
and fish templates for the children to share.

Directions:
1. Paint dark blue wave patterns on blue
construction paper.
2. Break Styrofoam® scraps into small pieces and
glue them on the blue paper to resemble icebergs.
3. Use the seal template to trace and cut out
two seal heads from gray paper. Add eyes,
a nose, whiskers, and a mouth with a marker.
4. Use the fish templates to trace and cut
out fish heads and tails from silver paper.
Add eyes, mouths, and scales with a marker.
5. Glue the seals and fish on the blue
background, bobbing about between
the icebergs.

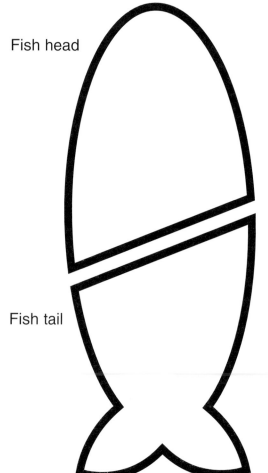

Fish head

Fish tail

Seal

Dogsled Team

Materials For Each Child:
1 sheet of 9" x 12" brown construction paper
½ sheet of 9" x 12" gray construction paper
1 husky template, to share
4 craft sticks
a small, rectangular container, such as a
   French fry container
black marker, pencil, scissors, and glue

Class Preparations:
Use the pattern below to make husky
templates for the children to share.

Directions:
1. Use the template to trace and cut out
two gray construction-paper huskies.
Use a marker to add eyes, noses, and fur.
2. Cut pieces of brown paper to cover
the sides of the container. Glue them on.
3. Glue two craft sticks to the bottom of
the container to make runners for your sled.
4. Glue one end of another craft stick to
the near side of the sled and the other end
to a husky cutout.
5. Glue a fourth craft stick to the far side
of the sled and to the other husky.
6. Now have the huskies pull the sled!

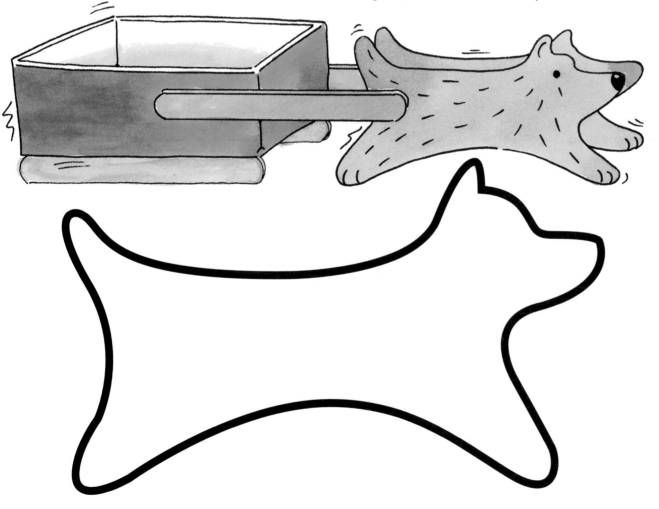

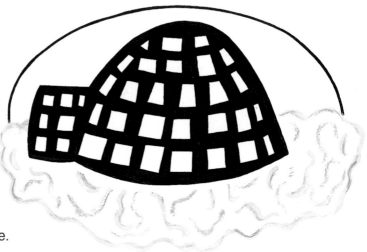

Igloo Collage

Materials For Each Child
1 sheet of 9" x 12" black construction paper
1 sheet of 9" x 12" white construction paper
½ sheet of 9" x 12" white drawing paper
1 igloo template, to share
cotton batting
pencil
scissors and glue

Class Preparations:
Use the pattern on the opposite page to make igloo templates for the children to share.

Directions:
1. Use the template to trace and cut out an igloo from black construction paper.
2. Draw and cut out an oval of white construction paper bigger than the igloo.
3. Cover the lower half of the oval with cotton batting, to look like snow.
4. Cut white drawing paper into ice-cube shapes. Glue these over the igloo in lines, putting narrower shapes around the edges.
5. Glue the igloo to the snowy background.

Ice Breaking Up

Materials For Each Child:
1 sheet of 9" x 12" white construction paper
Styrofoam® scraps
blue tempera paint
sponge, scissors, and glue

Class Preparations:
Cut each child's paper so that the top measures 9" and the bottom 12", to make the shape shown. Show the children pictures of the polar ice cap.

Directions:
1. Use a sponge to lightly dab blue paint all over the paper.
2. Cut Styrofoam® into different-sized jagged shapes.
3. Glue the Styrofoam® pieces on the paper. Place the biggest pieces close together at the top; then space out the smaller pieces more as you work down the paper.

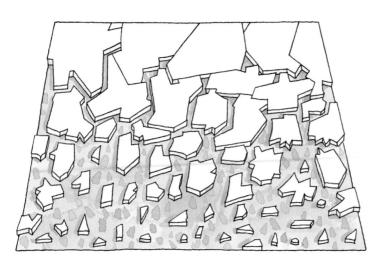

Use with Igloo Collage
on page 64.

Polar Bear On Ice

Materials For Each Child:
½ sheet of 9" x 12" blue construction paper
2 sheets of 9" x 12" white drawing paper
1 polar-bear head and 1 polar-bear body
   template, to share
black marker, pencil, eraser, and glue

Class Preparations:
Use the patterns on the opposite page to
make polar-bear body and head templates
for the children to share. Cut a piece of
9" x 6" blue construction paper for each child.

Directions:
1. Use the templates to trace a polar bear body
and head on white drawing paper. Tear carefully
along the lines.
2. Tear a curved shape from another sheet of
white paper to resemble an iceberg, as shown.
3. Glue the iceberg on the blue paper. Then glue
on the polar bear body so that it is standing on
the iceberg. Glue the head on the body, as
shown; then erase any pencil lines.
4. Use a marker to add eyes, a nose, and claws.

Icicle Bulletin-Board Trim

Materials For Each Child:
2 pieces of 12" x 9" white tissue paper
1 piece of 12" x 9" aluminum foil
glitter
soft pencil, scissors, and glue

Directions:
1. Lay one piece of tissue paper on a desk,
then lay the foil on top and cover with the other
piece of tissue paper. Line up the edges.
2. Use a soft pencil to carefully draw a row of
jagged icicles along the top piece of tissue paper.
Then cut out the icicles through all three layers.
3. Pull the bottom two layers down a little
so they can both be seen below the top
tissue-paper layer. Glue the three layers
together in this position. Allow to dry. 🅗
4. Dab glue on the tips of the white
tissue-paper icicles and sprinkle on glitter.
5. Decorate the bulletin board with the icicles. 🅣

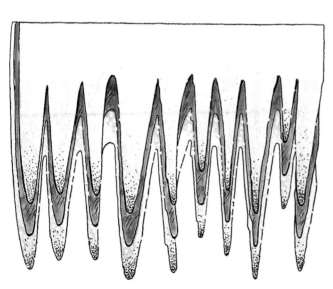

Use with Polar Bear On Ice
on page 66.

Seal In The Icy Water

Materials For Each Child:
1/2 sheet of 9" x 12" tagboard
1/4 sheet 9" x 12" gray construction paper
1 piece of 9" x 6" aluminum foil
2 wiggle eyes
black marker and colored crayons
glue, tape, pencil, and scissors

Class Preparations:
For each child, cut a piece of 9" x 6"
tagboard and a piece of 6" x 4 1/2"
gray paper. Cut foil to size.

Directions:
1. Glue the foil to one side of the tagboard.
2. Draw a jagged star shape for the ice on
the other side of the tagboard; then cut it out.
3. Draw a seal head shape, as shown,
on gray paper and cut it out. Use a marker
to draw on the seal's nose, mouth, and
whiskers. Use crayons to add patterned skin.
4. Glue on wiggle eyes.
5. Glue the seal to the center of the icy
background.

Polar Bear Puppet

Materials For Each Child:
2 pieces of 9" x 12" white felt
scraps of black and pink felt
1 polar bear template
needle, pins, and thread
black marker, scissors, and glue

Class Preparations:
Duplicate the polar bear pattern on the
opposite page on tagboard and cut out
to make a template for each child.

Directions:
1. Use the template to trace and cut out
two white felt bear shapes.
2. Pin the pieces together, lining up the edges.
Draw the stitching lines on one side.
3. Thread the needle; then sew along the
stitching lines, leaving the bottom open. Ⓗ
4. Cut out small circles for eyes, a larger one
for the nose, and eight pointed claws from the
black felt. Cut out a tongue from pink felt.
5. Glue the features in place on the puppet.
6. Use a marker to draw on the bear's mouth.

Use with Polar Bear
Puppet on page 68.

winter

Have the children think of all the things they associate with snow. These projects will help them along.

Footprints In The Snow

Materials For Each Child:
1 sheet of 12" x 18" white construction paper
black tempera paint in a shallow dish
printing tools for pig, human, bear, bird,
  and duck footprints, to share
scissors

Class Preparations:
Provide children with pictures of animal
footprints. Make printing tools of each
type of footprint for the children to share.
  For a pig, cut a carrot widthwise, then
cut a "V" in the edge of the cut surface.
  For a human, cut a potato in half
lengthwise. Use one half for the left foot
and the other for the right.
  For bear, bird, and duck prints,
use the patterns above to cut out the
shapes from tagboard; then glue each
one to the blunt end of a pencil.

Directions:
1. Dip one of the printing
tools into paint and use it
to print a line of footprints
across the paper.
2. Using a different printing
tool, make another row of
footprints next to the first.
Continue until the paper
is covered.
3. Allow to dry; then cut
the paper into a random
shape, as shown, to make
a patch of snow.

Duck   Bird

Bear

Ski Race

Materials For Each Child:

1 sheet of 9" x 12" white tagboard
¼ sheet of 9" x 12" white tagboard,
   with 2 skier outlines
½ sheet of 9" x 12" green construction paper
1 tree template, to share
colored markers, pencil, scissors, and glue

Class Preparations:

Use the pattern below to make tree templates for the children to share. For each child, duplicate the skier pattern twice on white tagboard.

Directions:

1. Draw a jagged line for the mountainside from the top left to the bottom right of the tagboard; then cut it out.

2. Draw two sloping ski runs with a pencil. Carefully push scissors through the tagboard at one end of each run and cut along the line, but don't cut right to the edges. **H**

3. Color and cut out the two skiers.

4. Use the tree template to trace and cut out several trees from green paper. Glue the trees on the mountainside.

5. Push the tab at the bottom of each skier through one of the ski runs. Now challenge a friend to a race. Move the skiers using the tabs.

Tree

Skier

Snow Cloud

Materials For Each Child:
¹/₂ sheet of 9" x 12" white construction paper,
  with cloud outline
4 pieces of white thread, about 12" in length
cotton batting
white tissue-paper scraps
a needle and a piece of string
glue, tape, and scissors

Class Preparations:
For each child, duplicate the cloud pattern
on white construction paper.

Directions:
1. Cut out the cloud shape. Glue fluffy
pieces of cotton batting all over the cloud.
2. Thread the needle and tie a double knot
at the end of the thread. ⓗ
3. Crumple small pieces of tissue paper
into balls. Use the needle and thread to
make a chain of five tissue-paper balls,
leaving a gap between each. Glue in place.
4. Repeat with three more lengths of thread.
5. Tape the threads to the back
of the cloud. Tape a piece
of string to the top
of the cloud to
hang it up.

Snowy Mobile

Materials For Each Child:

1 sheet of 9" x 12" green construction paper,
  with 5 tree outlines
1 sheet of 9" x 12" white drawing paper
2 clean, wooden skewers
5 pieces of white thread, 8" in length
1 piece of string
scissors, glue, and silver glitter
hole puncher to share

Class Preparations:

For each child, use string to tie the skewers
together in the middle to make a cross.
Duplicate the tree pattern below right five
times on green construction paper.

Directions:

1. Cut out the five trees; then use a hole
puncher to make a hole in the top of each tree. Ⓗ
2. Spread glue on the edges of each tree and
sprinkle on glitter. Allow to dry. Tie a piece of
thread through the hole in each tree.
3. Tear 30 small circles of white drawing paper.
Glue three pieces along each thread, about
1" apart; then glue another piece to the back
of each, sandwiching the thread in between.
Allow to dry.
4. Tie one thread to each end of the skewers
and one to the center. Ⓗ
5. Tie a length of string to the center of
the mobile and hang it up. Ⓣ

Window Watchers

Materials For Each Child:
¹/₆ sheet of 9" x 12" white construction paper
6 strips of black construction paper, 4¹/₂" x ¹/₄"
tempera paints in skin tones,
   in shallow containers
colored markers and glue

Class Preparations:
For each child, cut a piece of white paper
measuring 4¹/₂" x 4" and six strips of black
paper measuring 4¹/₂" x ¹/₄".

Directions:
1. Dip your finger or thumb into paint and
make five prints near the middle of the white
paper. Wash your hand and allow paint to dry.
2. Use markers to add features and
bobble hats to the faces.
3. Glue black construction-paper strips
across the window and around
the edges to make a
window frame.

Winter Count

Materials For Each Child:
1 brown paper bag
1 bucket filled with cold tea, to share
waterproof black marker
pencil, colored crayons, and newspaper

Class Preparations:
Talk about the Plains Indians' tradition of making
a count every winter to record all the events of
the past year. Provide buckets full of cold tea.

Directions:
1. Tear the bag into a rough shape
to resemble a piece of buffalo skin.
2. Think about the things you and your family
did in the last year that are important to you.
Use a pencil to draw pictures of these events
on the bag. You could draw numbers to show
the ages of family members on their birthdays,
a train to remind you of a trip, your favorite toy,
or family pets.
3. Trace over the pencil lines with the marker,
and color with crayons, pressing heavily.
4. Crumple up the paper and dip it into the
tea bucket. Remove the paper and spread it
out to dry on newspaper. It will soon look like
old leather.

Welcome the New Year with these activities inspired by different traditions from around the world.

New Year Pig

· · · · · · · · · · · · · · · · · · ·

Materials For Each Child:
1 piece of self-hardening modeling clay,
   about the size of a tennis ball
1 fork or toothpick
1 coin
1 piece of pipe cleaner, 3" long
pink and black tempera paints and paintbrushes

Class Preparations:
Cut pipe cleaners to size for each child.
Provide a pot of water for the children to share.
Talk about the Austrian tradition of giving children
on New Year's Day a toy pig with a coin or
four-leaf clover in its mouth for good luck.

Directions:
1. Make two clay balls, each about the size of a
ping-pong ball. Press your thumb into the center
of each ball and pinch the clay around it to make
a hollow pot shape, as shown (A).
2. Put a little water on the rim of each pot and
join the pots together to make the pig's body, as
shown (B). Score across the seam with a fork or
toothpick, then gently smooth with your finger. (H)
3. Roll four short, thick clay sausages for legs
and attach them to the pig, scoring across the
seam in the same way that you did for the pots.
4. Add a clay snout and ears. Curl the pipe
cleaner to make a tail and push it into the pig.
5. Press the coin into the clay beneath
the pig's snout. Allow the pig to dry.
6. Paint the pig pink and paint
on black eyes, nostrils,
a mouth, and hoofs.

B

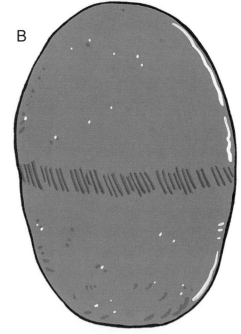

A

Promise Scroll

Materials For Each Child:
1 sheet of 9" x 12" white drawing paper
1 wet teabag
1 ribbon, 12" in length
black fine-tip marker

Class Preparations:
Talk with your class about the tradition of making New Year's resolutions. Put one teabag into warm water for each child. Provide examples of old scripts. Have a large box with a lid ready.

Directions:
1. Tear around the edges of a sheet of drawing paper. Dab a teabag all over; then allow to dry.

2. Use a marker to write New Year's resolutions on the paper. Add old-fashioned curls and squiggles and sign your name at the bottom.
3. Fold and unfold the paper several times. Roll the paper into a scroll and tie with a ribbon. (H)
4. Put the scrolls in a box, seal, and label with a date near the end of term. On that date, open the box and see how many resolutions you've kept. (T)

Chinese New Year Dragon Streamer

Materials For Each Child:
2 sheets of 9" x 12" white tagboard, with outlines of 2 dragon heads and 2 flames
1 strip of posterboard, 5" in length
12 red and yellow crepe-paper streamers, 10" in length
green and red tempera paints
paintbrushes and black marker
scissors, tape, and glue

Class Preparations:
For each child, duplicate the dragon patterns on page 77 twice on white tagboard.

Directions:
1. Cut out the dragon heads and flames. Turn a head and a flame over to face the opposite way, and paint the heads green and the flames red.

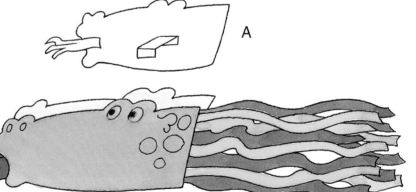

A

2. Allow to dry; then glue a flame to the plain side of each head to appear out of the mouth. Use a marker to add black eyes, nostrils, and scales.
3. Fold back a small flap at each end of the posterboard strip. Tape each flap to the back of one dragon head, as shown (A), to make a handle. (H)
4. Glue streamers to the plain side of the back of each head.
5. Allow to dry; then hold the head up and run, so that the streamers look like a dragon's body.

Use with Chinese New Year
Dragon Streamer on page 76.

Dragon
head

Dragon
flame

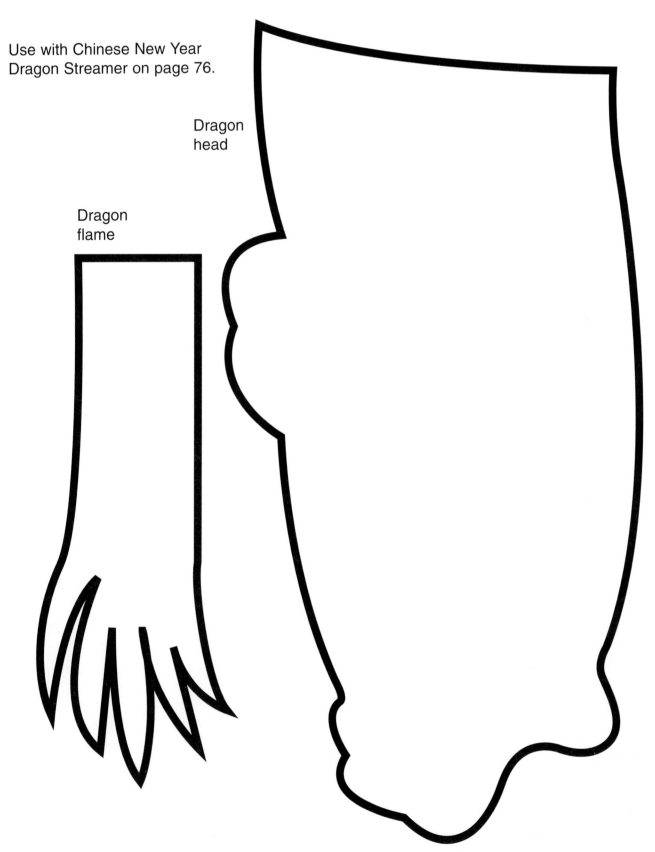

Chinese Lucky Money

Materials For Each Child:
½ sheet of 9" x 12" red construction paper,
  with envelope outline
gold and silver paper scraps
coins to share
black crayon
gold marker
colored tape, scissors, and glue

Class Preparations:
For each child, enlarge the pattern below
to fit on a piece of 9" x 6" red construction
paper. Provide examples of Chinese
writing for the children to copy.

Directions:
1. Cut out the envelope outline. Fold the paper
along the dotted lines and glue the bottom and
side flaps. Leave the top open.

2. Write "Happy New Year" on the envelope
in gold, and decorate with Chinese characters.
3. Place a scrap of gold or silver paper over a
coin. Rub a black crayon gently over the paper.
Repeat with the other side of the coin. Cut out
both shapes and glue them back to back.
Make several coins in the same way.
4. Put the coins in the envelope and seal the
top flap with colored tape. Give the envelope
to a friend as a New Year gift.

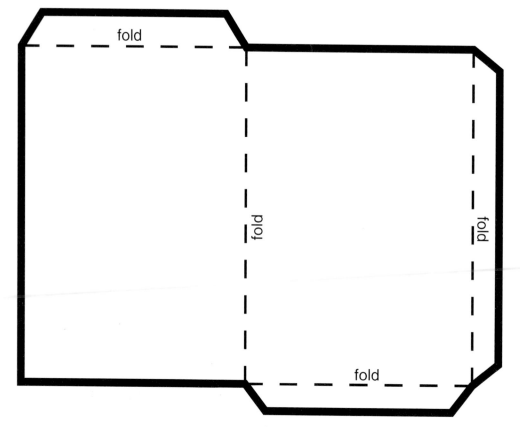

> Don't forget Martin Luther King's birthday on January 15th, and Burns Night on the 25th!

Shake Hands!

Materials For Each Child:
2 half sheets of 9" x 12" tagboard in contrasting skin tones
2 strips of colored construction paper, 1" x 3"
1 brass fastener
pencil, scissors, and glue

Class Preparations:
Cut sheets of 9" x 12" skin-tone tagboard in half widthwise and provide each child with two pieces of tagboard in contrasting colors.

Directions:
1. Draw around each of your hands on separate pieces of tagboard and cut out.
2. Glue strips of colored construction paper to the wrists, to make cuffs.
3. Overlap the hands in a handshake position and push a brass fastener through the overlapping part to secure. Ⓗ

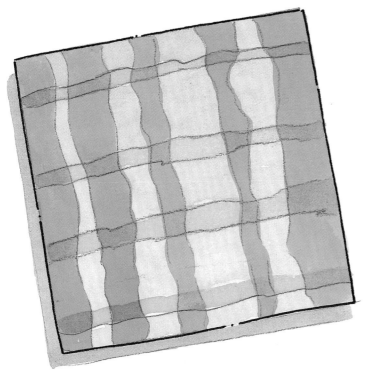

Tartan Plaid

Materials For Each Child:
1 square of white construction paper, 6" x 6"
¹/₂ sheet of 12" x 18" colored tissue paper
scissors and glue

Class Preparations:
Provide samples of various Scottish tartans and explain to the children that Burns Night is a traditional Scottish celebration. Together, cut or tear three different colors of tissue paper into narrow strips, 6" in length.

Directions:
1. Glue rows of tissue-paper strips across the construction-paper square, alternating the colors.
2. Glue more strips of alternating colors down the paper on top of the first strips. Leave a gap about the same width as a strip between each one. Allow to dry.
3. Pin all the tartan squares together on a bulletin board, to make a patchwork display. Ⓣ

Try these unusual ways of surprising your loved ones on Valentine's Day. They'll keep everyone guessing!

Woven Hearts

. . . .

Materials For Each Child:
1/2 sheet each of 9" x 12" yellow and blue
   construction paper
1 template
1 narrow ribbon, approximately 3" in length
pencil and ruler
scissors and glue

Class Preparations:
Use the pattern on the opposite page to make a template for each child. Use a pencil to mark on the two lines. Cut sheets of construction paper in half widthwise and give each child two half sheets of paper in different colors.

Directions:
1. Fold a piece of construction paper in half. Place the straight edge of the template along the fold, trace around it and cut out the shape. Do not cut along the fold. Repeat with the other piece of construction paper.
2. Use a pencil and ruler to mark on the two lines; then cut along them.
3. Keeping each piece folded, weave the blue piece through the yellow piece. Put the two sides of the first strip of the blue piece around the first strip of the yellow piece, then push it through the middle of the second strip, then around the third strip, as shown (A). Weave the second strip of the blue piece through the first strip of the yellow piece, then around the second strip, then through the third strip (B). Weave the third strip of the blue piece as you did for the first strip (C). ⊕
4. Glue one end of a ribbon inside one side of the heart; then glue the other end to the other side. Hang up the heart. ⊕

A

B

C

Valentine Bookmark

Materials For Each Child:

1 strip of red or gold construction paper,
  2" x 6"
1 narrow ribbon, 10" in length
construction-paper, tissue-paper, and
  cellophane scraps in valentine colors
3 heart templates, to share
hole puncher to share
pencil, scissors, and glue

Class Preparations:

Use the heart patterns below right to make
templates in different sizes for the children
to share. To make a bookmark for each
child, cut a 2" x 6" strip of red or gold
construction paper.

Use with Woven
Hearts on
page 80.

Directions:

1. Cut one end of the construction-paper
strip into a point for your bookmark.
2. Use a hole puncher to punch
a hole in the pointed end. Ⓗ
3. Fold the ribbon in half and thread
the loop through the hole. Then
thread the two loose ends of
the ribbon through the loop
and pull gently to secure. Ⓗ
4. Use the templates to trace and
cut out different-sized hearts from
different materials. Glue them
to one side of your bookmark.
5. Write a valentine message
on the back of the bookmark.

Use with Valentine
Bookmark on this
page and Valentine
Wrappings on
page 82.

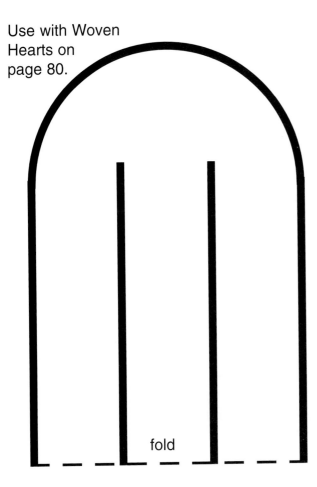

fold

Valentine Wrappings

Materials For Each Child:
½ sheet of 12" x 18" pink tissue paper
1 large and 1 small heart template,
   to share
1 small gift or card
dark pink construction-paper scrap
Styrofoam® scrap
red tempera paint in a shallow container
pencil and marker
scissors, glue, and tape

Class Preparations:
Use the smallest and largest heart patterns
on page 81 to make heart templates for the
children to share.

Directions:
1. Use the small heart template to trace and
cut out a Styrofoam® heart. Glue the heart
on the blunt end of a pencil and allow to dry.

2. Dip the heart into red paint and print
onto pink tissue paper. Print lots of hearts
in the same way. Allow to dry.
3. Wrap the paper around a valentine's gift
or card. Secure with tape.
4. Use the large heart template to trace and cut
out a dark pink construction-paper heart. Write
your valentine's name on the heart and glue to
the overlap of the paper as a finishing touch.

Love You!

Materials For Each Child:
1 sheet of 12" x 18" construction paper
wax crayon
tempera paint
paintbrush

Directions:
1. Use a wax crayon to draw lots of hearts
on one side of a sheet of construction paper.
2. Paint all over the same side of the
construction paper. Allow to dry.
3. Use the paper to wrap a valentine gift.

Valentine Mobile

Materials For Each Child:
1 sheet of 9" x 12" red construction paper
1 large and 1 small heart template, to share
colored construction-paper and fabric scraps
strong thread and glue
pencil, colored markers, and scissors

Class Preparations:
Use the patterns on page 84 to make heart templates for the children to share.

Directions:
1. Use the larger template to trace and cut out two red construction-paper hearts.
2. Glue paper and fabric scraps on one heart. Write "I love..." on the other heart.
3. Use the smaller template to trace and cut out ten hearts from construction-paper scraps. Draw pictures of people you love on five hearts and write their names on each of the other hearts.
4. Spread glue on the backs of the 'picture' hearts, lay the end of a length of thread on each; then lay the matching 'name' hearts on top.
5. Spread glue on the back of the large "I love…" heart. Position the ends of the five threads, plus a loop of thread at the top. Press on the collage heart.
Allow to dry; then hang up.

Valentine Puzzle

Materials For Each Child:
½ sheet of 9" x 12" red construction paper
1 heart template, to share
envelope or box
colored sequins
colored markers, scissors, and glue

Class Preparations:
Use the large pattern on page 84 to make templates for the children to share.

Directions:
1. Use the template to trace and cut out a red construction-paper heart.
2. Use markers to draw flowers on one side of the heart.
3. Glue sequins all around the edge.
4. Write your valentine's message on the back.
5. Cut the heart into five or six pieces, carefully avoiding the sequins. Put the pieces in an envelope or a box and send them to your valentine. Will he or she be able to solve the puzzle and work out who sent it?

winter

Use with Valentine Mobile
and Valentine Puzzle,
both on page 83.

Use with Valentine Mobile
on page 83.

spring

Blowing In The Wind

Materials For Each Child:
1 sheet of 12" x 18" white construction paper
1 sheet of 9" x 12" white construction paper,
   with clothes outlines
3 wooden skewers, about 7" in length
1 piece of string, 20" in length
a cotton ball
blue and green tempera paints and paintbrushes
colored markers, scissors, and glue

Class Preparations:
For each child, duplicate the patterns on the
opposite page on white construction paper.

Directions:
1. Paint the top half of the construction paper
blue, for the sky, and the bottom half green, for
grass. Allow to dry.
2. Glue the skewers on the paper, as shown.
3. Glue the string across the tops of the
skewers, letting it sag slightly in between. Ⓗ
4. Cut out the clothes and color with markers
on both sides. Fold over the tabs of each cutout
and dab glue in the fold. Hang on the string and
press the tabs down.
5. Pull at the cotton ball to make a wispy cloud.
Glue it to the sky to complete your windy scene.

Cherry Tree

Materials For Each Child:
½ sheet of 12" x 18" green crepe paper
red construction-paper scraps
a clay flowerpot
sand or potting soil
a branched twig
a bottle top
scissors, string, and glue

Class Preparations:
Have the children collect branched twigs (one for
each child or a large one for the whole class).

Directions:
1. Fill a pot with sand or soil and push the twig
into it to make a mini tree.
2. Cut green crepe paper into short strips.
Tie each strip around a branch of the twig to
make leaves. Ⓗ
3. Use a bottle top as a template to trace and
cut small circles from red construction paper, for
cherries. Cut short pieces of string and glue a
cherry to each end. Hang each pair of cherries
over a branch and
glue in place.

86

Use with Blowing In The Wind on page 86.

Why not welcome spring by making colorful flowers? Shoots are beginning to sprout at this time of year.

A

Sunflower Pins

Materials For Each Child:
1 strip of yellow crepe paper, 1½" x 18"
1 yellow posterboard circle, 2" in diameter
dark brown tissue-paper scraps
safety pin and masking tape
marker and glue

Class Preparations:
Use a jar lid to trace and cut out a
2" posterboard circle for each child.
Cut strips of yellow crepe paper.

Directions:
1. Accordion-fold a crepe-paper strip into sections about ¾" wide. Draw a petal shape on the top section, as shown (A). Cut out the shape to make lots of petals. (H)
2. Glue the end of each petal around the edge of the back of the posterboard circle, as shown.
3. Tear dark brown tissue paper into small pieces and crumple into balls. Glue to the front of the circle until it is covered.
4. Tape a safety pin to the back of the circle and wear your sunflower to welcome spring!

Spring Garland

Materials For Each Child:
2½ sheets of 9" x 12" construction paper in different pastel colors
1 flower template
1 piece of narrow ribbon, 30" in length
collage materials, such as colored paper, raffia, felt, and buttons
pencil, scissors, and glue

Class Preparations:
Use the pattern on the opposite page to make a flower template for each child.

Directions:
1. Use the template to trace and cut out ten construction-paper flowers in pastel colors.
2. Glue on collage materials to decorate one side of each flower.
3. Glue two flowers back to back in the center of the ribbon, sandwiching the ribbon between them. Overlap the flowers so all the petals are visible. Repeat with the other flowers. (H)
4. Tie your garland around your neck, or use it to decorate the classroom. (H)

Carnation Centerpiece

Materials For Each Child:

1 paper plate, 7" in diameter
6 strips of brightly colored crepe paper, 12" x 3"
green construction-paper scraps
green tempera paint
paintbrush
pencil
scissors
glue

Directions:

1. Cut out the center of the paper plate to leave a circular ring (see Practical Tips, page 4).

2. Paint the ring green; then allow to dry.

3. To make a flower, spread glue along one long edge of a brightly colored crepe-paper strip and roll up tightly. Cut long slits down the tube, through all the layers, as shown (A). Then pull the cut strips out and bend down (B). Make six flowers and glue them on the ring.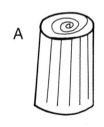

4. Draw leaf shapes on green construction-paper scraps and cut out. Glue the leaves on your ring, between the flowers, as a finishing touch.

Use with Spring Garland on page 88.

A

B

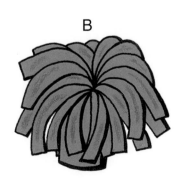

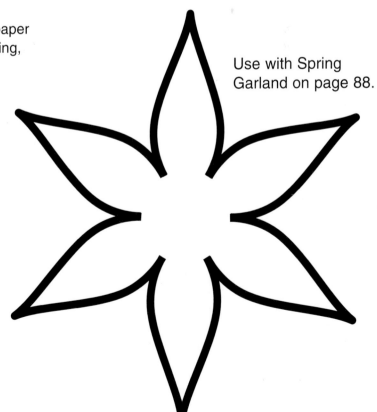

Printing Pots

• • • • • • • • • • • • • • • • • • •

Materials For Each Child:
3 apple, orange, or lemon seeds
a clay flowerpot, about 5" tall
apple, orange, or lemon printing blocks, to share
potting soil and water
plastic wrap
a rubber band
a saucer
various colors of tempera paint
   in shallow containers
paintbrushes

Class Preparations:
To make a printing block, first trace one of the patterns on the opposite page on thin sponge and cut out. Then fold a strip of posterboard, about 9" in length, into three sections and tape the ends together to make a triangle. Glue the sponge shape to one side of the triangle, as shown (A). Make several printing blocks for each fruit. To make a half-fruit printing block, cut out a whole fruit from sponge; then cut in half.

Have each child collect orange, apple, or lemon seeds. Wash and dry the seeds.

Directions:
1. Paint the outside of a flowerpot all over in one color and allow to dry.
2. Use a printing block that matches the fruit your seeds come from. Dip the block into paint and press onto the side of the pot. Print all around the pot.
3. Use a paintbrush to add details such as leaves and seeds. Allow to dry.
4. Fill the pot with soil and push in three seeds to about 1" deep. Push a little soil over the seeds. Water the soil and cover the top of the pot with plastic wrap. Secure with a rubber band. 🅗
5. Place the pot on a saucer on a sunny windowsill. When shoots appear, remove the plastic wrap and keep the soil moist.

A

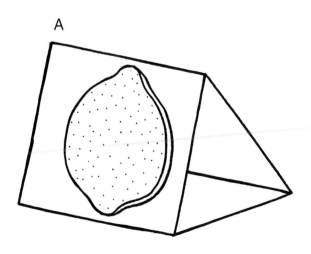

Lemon

Use with Printing Pots on page 90.

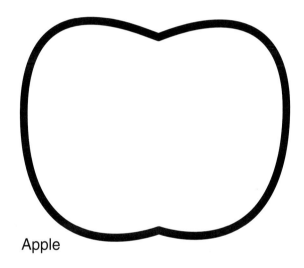

Apple

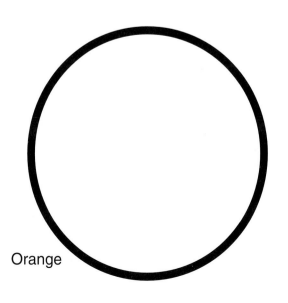

Orange

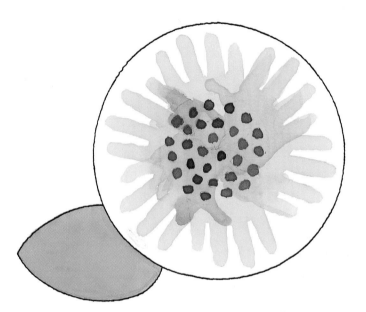

Sunny Sunflower

Materials For Each Child:
1 paper plate, 7" in diameter
1/4 sheet of green construction paper
1 jar lid, 3" in diameter, to share
yellow and brown tempera paints
   in shallow dishes
pencil and scissors

Class Preparations:
For each child, cut a piece of 4½" x 6" green construction paper. Provide paper towels and soapy water to wash up.

Directions:
1. Dip the palm of one of your hands into yellow paint and print all around the paper plate with your palm in the center; then wash your hands. Allow the paint to dry.
2. Use a jar lid to trace a circle in the center of the plate.
3. Dip a fingertip in brown paint and fill the circle with fingerprints; then wash your hands.
4. Draw a leaf on green construction paper and cut out; then glue to the back of the plate.
5. Staple the flowers to a bulletin board to make a field of sunny sunflowers. Ⓣ

Chicks and eggs make a perfect theme for Easter cards. Try these cute ideas!

Spring Blossoms

Materials For Each Child:
1 empty yogurt container
1 piece of colored construction paper,
 large enough to cover the container
4 bare twigs
pink and white tissue-paper scraps
green construction-paper scraps
modeling clay, about the size of a ping-pong ball
green crayon, pencil, scissors, and glue

Class Preparations:
Have the children collect twigs.

Directions:
1. Cut a piece of colored construction paper to fit around your container; then glue to secure.
2. To make blossoms, tear pink and white tissue paper into squares, about 2" x 2", and crumple into balls. Glue six or seven blossoms onto each twig.
3. Draw 15 small leaves on green construction paper and cut out. Use a green crayon to draw veins on each leaf; then glue the leaves on the twigs.
4. Put a piece of modeling clay in the bottom of the yogurt container. Arrange your blossoming twigs in the clay.

Easter Chick Card

Materials For Each Child:
1/2 sheet of 9" x 12" white construction paper,
 with egg outline
1/4 sheet of 9" x 12" yellow construction paper,
 with chick outline
a brass fastener
gummed-paper scraps
colored markers, pencil, scissors, and glue

Class Preparations:
For each child, duplicate the egg pattern on the opposite page on white construction paper and the chick pattern on yellow construction paper.

Directions:
1. Cut out the egg. Draw a zigzag line across the middle and cut along it.
2. Cut out gummed-paper shapes and stick them on the front of the egg halves.
3. Color and cut out the chick; then write an Easter greeting on the back.
4. Glue the bottom of the chick to the back of the zigzag edge of one egg half.
5. Attach the two halves of the egg at one side with a brass fastener, so that the egg can be opened and closed for an Easter surprise! 🄷

92

Use with Easter Chick Card on page 92 and Easter Egg Card on page 94.

Use with Easter Chick Card on page 92 and Chirpy Spring Chick on page 94.

Chirpy Spring Chick

Materials For Each Child:

1 sheet of 9" x 12" colored construction paper
1/4 sheet of yellow construction paper,
   with chick outline
black and orange markers
pencil, scissors, and glue

Class Preparations:

For each child, duplicate the chick pattern on page 93 on yellow construction paper.

Directions:

1. Fold the colored construction paper in half to make a card. Cut two slits in the folded edge, as shown (A). Fold the flap forward, then flatten it down again.

2. Open the card. Push the cut section forward from behind, to make it stand out like a step.

3. Cut out the chick and use markers to color the features.

4. Glue the chick to the pop-up section of the card, as shown.

5. Use a marker to draw the chick's feet on the card. Write a greeting on the outside of the card.

Easter Egg Card

Materials For Each Child:

1 sheet of 9" x 12" colored construction paper
1/2 sheet of 9" x 12" white construction paper,
   with egg outline
tempera paints and paintbrushes
pencil, scissors, and glue

Class Preparations:

For each child, duplicate the egg pattern on page 93 on white construction paper.

Directions:

1. Fold the colored paper in half to make a card. Cut out the egg.

2. Trace around the egg on the front of the card. Cut out to leave an egg-shaped frame (see Practical Tips, page 4).

3. Fold the paper egg in half lengthwise and open it out again. Drip different colors of paint onto one half; then fold the egg to sandwich the paint. Rub the top surface with your hand. Unfold the egg and allow to dry.

4. Close the card. Draw a line around the inside of the frame, on the inside of the card. Open the card and use the line as a guide to glue on the paper egg.

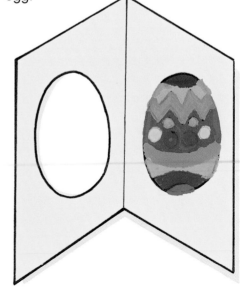

Little Chick Napkin Ring

Materials For Each Child:

1 sheet of 9" x 12" yellow construction paper,
   with 2 chick outlines and 2 wing outlines
cardboard tube, 2" in length
tempera paints, including orange and black
paintbrushes
scissors, tape, and glue

Class Preparations:

For each child, duplicate the chick and wing
patterns on the right twice on yellow construction
paper. Cut cardboard tubes into 2" lengths.

Directions:

1. Cut out the outlines of two chicks and two
wings. Lay the chicks with one facing left and
one facing right. Glue a wing onto each chick.
2. Paint a black eye and an orange beak
on each chick.
3. Paint the tube in a different color. Allow to dry.
4. Tape one chick to each side of the tube, as
shown, with the wings on the outside. 🄗
5. Use the chicks to hold your
napkin at Easter.

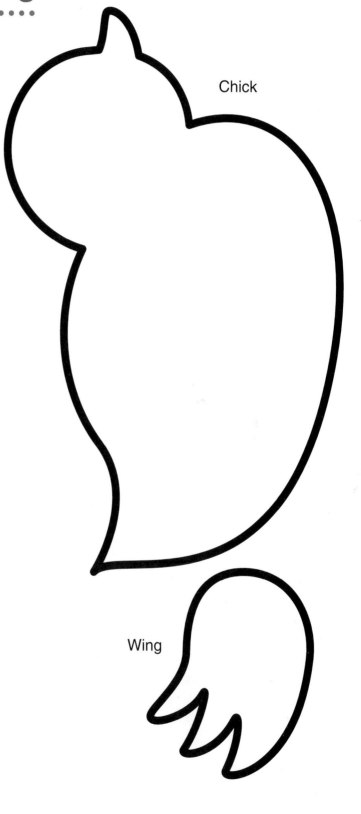

Chick

Wing

Eggshell Armadillo Card

Materials For Each Child:
1 sheet of 9" x 12" tan construction paper
1 armadillo template, to share
1 wiggle eye
shell of one egg
brown tempera paint and paintbrush
black markers, pencil, scissors, and glue

Class Preparations:
Hard boil one egg for each child and peel off the shell. Use the pattern below to make templates for the children to share.

Directions:
1. Fold a sheet of tan construction paper in half to make a card. Line up the top of the template with the fold and trace around the armadillo. ⊕ Cut out the shape, but do not cut along the fold.
2. Glue a wiggle eye on the front of the card and draw on features.
3. Spread glue on the armadillo's body and cover with pieces of eggshell. Press down on each piece to break the shell into tiny pieces, to make the armadillo's armor. Allow to dry.
4. Paint the armor brown and allow to dry.
5. Write an Easter greeting inside the card.

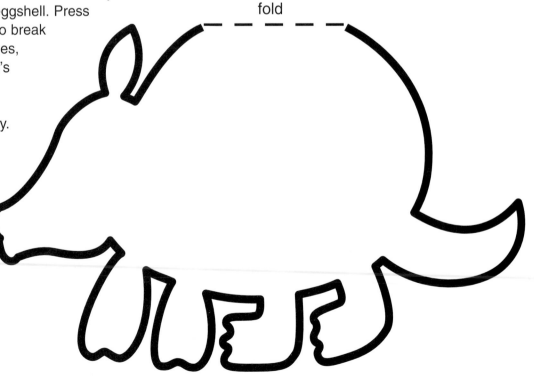

fold

Giant Eggs

Materials For Each Child:

1 balloon
1 old Easter card
1 piece of thread, about 6" in length
1 piece of string, about 12" in length
several sheets of newspaper
watered-down glue in a
   plastic container, to share
tempera paints
paintbrushes
pencil
scissors
tape

Class Preparations:

For this activity, you will need a collection of old Easter cards. For each child, blow up a balloon and knot the end. Mix equal parts of glue and water in plastic containers.

Directions:

1. Tear newspaper into strips. Dip the strips into watered-down glue and plaster onto the balloon, as shown (A). Do not cover the balloon completely—leave a large, round uncovered patch on one side (B). Allow to dry for about an hour.

2. Plaster on two more layers of newspaper strips, leaving each layer to dry, as in step 1; then allow to dry overnight.

3. Use a pencil to burst the balloon. Then pull the balloon out of the hole. Use scissors to trim the edges of the hole; then glue on newspaper strips to neaten. Allow to dry. 🅗

4. Paint the newspaper egg inside and out using bright colors.

5. Cut out a picture from an old Easter card. Tape one end of a piece of thread to the back of the figure and tape the other end inside the top of the egg.

6. Tape a piece of string to the top of the egg to hang your giant Easter egg.

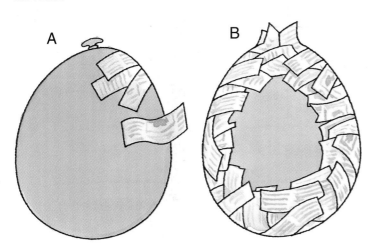

A   B

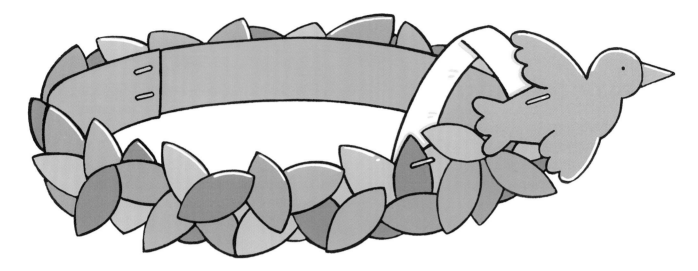

Easter Headbands

Materials For Each Child:
1 strip of green construction paper, 2" x 18"
1/4 sheet of 9" x 12" white construction paper,
   with bird outline
1 strip of plastic from a plastic bottle, 1/2" x 7"
green construction-paper scraps
stapler to share
colored markers
scissors and glue

Class Preparations:
For each child, use a craft knife to cut a 1/2" x 7"
strip from an empty plastic bottle or liquid
detergent bottle. Duplicate the bird pattern
on this page on white construction paper.

Directions:
1. Wrap the green paper strip around your head.
Keeping it in the same shape, remove from your
head and staple the ends together to make a
headband. Trim the ends if necessary. (H)
2. Draw leaves on green construction-paper
scraps and cut out; then glue them on the
headband, as shown. Allow to dry.
3. Use markers to color the bird. Then cut it out.
4. Staple the bird to one end of a plastic strip; then
staple the other end of the strip to the headband. (H)

Flying High

● ● ● ● ● ● ● ● ● ● ● ● ● ● ● ● ●

Materials For Each Child:
½ sheet of 9" x 12" colored tagboard
1 sheet of 9" x 12" construction paper
1 bird template, to share
a length of string
colored markers, pencil, scissors, and tape

Class Preparations:
Use the pattern below to make bird templates
for the children to share. Cut sheets of
tagboard into halves.

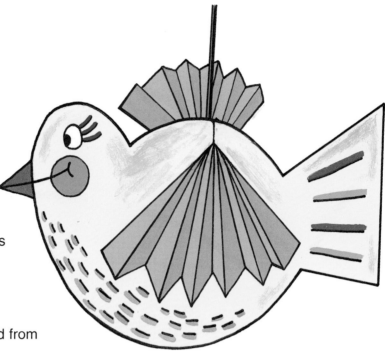

Directions:
1. Use a template to trace and cut out a bird from
tagboard. Decorate the body using markers.
2. Accordion-fold a sheet of construction
paper along its length.
3. Cut a vertical slit, about 1" in length,
in the top of the bird's body.
4. Push the folded
paper into the slit.
Open out
the folds to
resemble wings.
5. Tape string
to the top
of the bird
to hang.

Use with Little Lamb Mask
on page 101.

This project will turn your class into a flock of little lambs! Allow them to visit other classrooms as a surprise.

Little Lamb Mask

Materials For Each Child:
1 sheet of 9" x 12" white construction paper, with lamb mask outline
1 ear template, to share
pink fabric scraps and cotton batting
stapler to share, scissors, and glue

Class Preparations:
For each child, duplicate the mask pattern on page 100 on white construction paper. Use the ear pattern on page 100 to make templates for the children to share. Have a class supply of elastic ready.

Directions:
1. Cut out the lamb mask. Then, cut out the eye holes and cut along the nose line to make a flap (See Practical Tips, page 4). ⓗ
2. Use the ear template to trace and cut out two lamb's ears from pink fabric.
3. Staple the ears to the top of the mask. ⓗ
4. Cut a piece of elastic to fit around your head and staple to the sides of the mask. ⓗ
5. Glue pieces of cotton batting around the edge of the mask, using the line as a guide.
6. To complete your lamb outfit, wear the mask with white clothes and a long white sock for a tail.

Ice-Cream Cones

Materials For Each Child:
1/3 circle of white construction paper
1/2 sheet of 9" x 12" pastel copy paper
1/2 sheet of newspaper
watered-down light brown tempera paint
paintbrush
brown crayon
sugar sprinkles and a red pompom
scissors, tape, and glue

Class Preparations:
Use a pin and string to help you draw and cut out 9" circles from white construction paper. Cut each circle into thirds and give each child one segment. Cut a piece of 9" x 6" pastel copy paper for each child. Mix light brown paint with water to make it very runny.

Directions:
1. Use a brown crayon to draw a grid on the white paper segment; then, paint the paper light brown to create a wafer effect. Allow to dry.
2. Curl the paper to make a cone. Glue the outside edge to secure. ⓗ
3. Crumple the newspaper into a ball. Place the ball in the center of the pastel paper and gather up the corners. Wind tape around the corners; then glue this taped end into the cone to make ice-cream. ⓗ
4. Spread glue on the ice-cream and scatter on sugar sprinkles.
5. Glue on a red pompom to resemble a cherry.

Spring Lamb Card

Materials For Each Child:

¹/₂ sheet of 9" x 12" black construction paper

¹/₄ sheet of 9" x 12" white construction paper, with lamb outline

1 green construction-paper strip, with grass outline

¹/₄ sheet of 12" x 18" white tissue paper

scissors and glue

Class Preparations:

For each child, duplicate the lamb pattern below on white construction paper and the grass pattern on a strip of green construction paper.

Directions:

1. Fold the black paper in half to make a greetings card.

2. Cut out the lamb and grass.

3. Glue the lamb on the front of the black folded card in the center.

4. Glue the grass on the bottom of the card, to cover the lamb's feet.

5. Tear white tissue paper into small squares; then crumple to make balls. Glue the balls on the lamb's body to give your lamb a woolly coat.

Your youngsters can really spoil Mom on Mother's Day with these special handmade cards and gifts.

Pop-Up Mother's Day Card

Materials For Each Child:
1 sheet of 9" x 12" white construction paper,
   with Supermom and 4 flower outlines
1/3 sheet of 12" x 18" colored construction paper
1 strip of colored construction paper, 1 1/2" x 3"
crayons, scissors, and glue

Class Preparations:
For each child, cut a 6" x 12" piece and a
1 1/2" x 3" strip from colored construction paper.
Duplicate the Supermom and flower patterns
on page 104 on white construction paper. Give
each child one Supermom outline and four
flower outlines.

Directions:
1. Fold the colored construction-paper
rectangle in half to make a greetings card.
2. Fold the paper strip in half; then fold
back a small flap at each end. Glue
the flaps inside the card to make a step,
as shown (A). 🌀
3. Color and cut out the Supermom and the flowers.
4. Glue the Supermom's legs to the paper step,
as shown (B).
5. Glue the paper flowers on the front of the card
and write "Mom" in the center. Decorate around
the flowers with crayons.

B

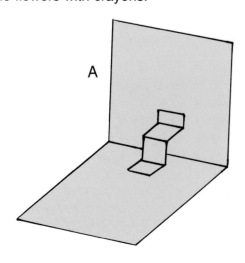

A

Use with Pop-Up Mother's Day Card on page 103.

Thumbs-Up Gift Wrap

Materials For Each Child:
1 sheet of 12" x 18" construction paper
1 piece of tagboard, 3" x 6"
a short piece of narrow ribbon
hole puncher to share
blue, red, and purple tempera paints
   in shallow containers
paintbrushes
long ruler
pencil and eraser

Directions:
1. Use a ruler and pencil to lightly draw lines across the paper, 3" apart; then draw lines down the paper, again 3" apart. Ⓗ
2. Make a red thumbprint on each place where the lines cross each other. This will give you a regular pattern.
3. Dip a paintbrush in blue paint and make a short brushstroke along one side of each thumbprint; then make a purple brushstroke on the opposite side. Allow to dry.
4. Erase the pencil lines.
5. Fold the small piece of tagboard in half to make a gift tag. Print and paint the tag to match.
6. Use a hole puncher to punch a hole in a corner by the fold of the tag. Thread a ribbon through. Ⓗ

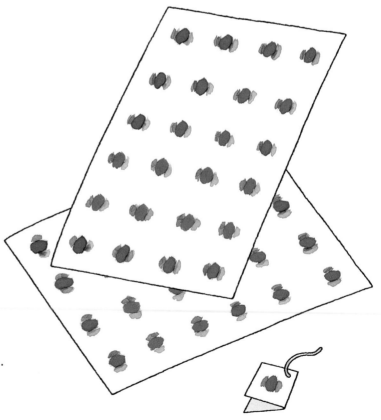

Mother's Day Bouquet

Materials For Each Child:
6 paper cups (3 oz.) in assorted colors
1 sheet of gift wrap or tissue paper
3 flexible straws
1 ribbon, 12" in length
colored tissue-paper scraps
pencil, scissors, and glue

Directions:
1. Cut the rim off each paper cup. Make cuts down the sides of each cup, all the way around, almost to the base. ⓗ
2. To make a flower, glue one cup inside another, different-colored cup; then bend back the cut strips to resemble petals.
3. Make two more flowers in the same way.
4. Use a pencil to make a hole in the center of each flower (see Practical Tips, page 4). Push a straw through the hole to make a stem. ⓗ
5. Crumple a scrap of tissue paper and glue on the center of each flower.
6. Wrap all the flowers in a sheet of gift wrap or tissue paper. Finally, tie a ribbon around your bouquet. ⓗ

A

Cactus Jewelry Tree

Materials For Each Child:
2 pieces of corrugated cardboard, about 9" x 12"
1 cactus template, to share
1 paper plate, 7" in diameter
newspaper
green and orange tempera paints
paintbrushes
pencil, scissors, tape, and glue

Class Preparations:
Duplicate the pattern on page 106 on tagboard to make templates for the children to share.

Directions:
1. Use the template to trace and cut out a cardboard cactus. Mark on the dotted line.
2. Trace around a plate on cardboard and cut out. Fold the cactus along the dotted line and tape this flap to the center of the circle cutout. ⓗ
3. Tear newspaper into pieces. Crumple into balls and tape them on the cactus and base.
4. Cover the cactus and base with a few layers of papier-mâché (see page 5). Allow to dry.
5. Paint the cactus green and the base orange. Allow to dry; then brush glue all over it.
6. Give to Mom as a unique Mother's Day gift!

Use with Cactus Jewelry
Tree on page 105.

fold

Your students will enjoy making creative artwork with a personal touch for Dad on Father's Day.

Father's Day Jacket Card

Materials For Each Child:

1 sheet of 9" x 12" white construction paper

self-hardening modeling clay,
   about the size of a ping-pong ball

red and blue tempera paints

paintbrushes

colored markers

black marker

pencil

scissors

double-sided tape

Directions:

1. Fold the paper in half, but don't crease it. Snip off the top corner (A) and open the paper flat again. ⬤

2. Fold in the two short edges of the paper to meet in the center and crease (B). ⬤

3. Open the card and draw a shirt and tie, a T-shirt, or whatever type of shirt your Dad wears, in the middle section (C). Use markers to color the shirt.

4. Close the card and draw a jacket design on the front of it with a pencil. Color with markers.

5. Mold the clay into a flat circle or shield. Allow the clay to dry; then paint the front blue with a red "S" for "Superdad."

6. Write a message to Dad on the inside of the jacket flaps. Then use double-sided tape to fix the "Superdad" badge to the front of the jacket.

A

B

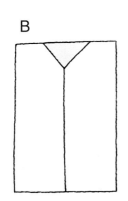

C

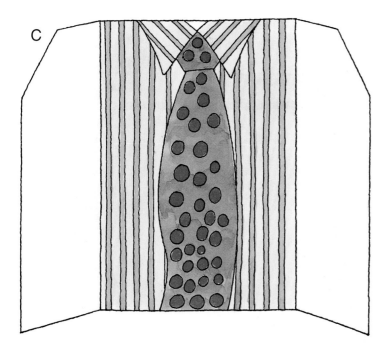

Father's Day Pen Holder

Materials For Each Child:

½ sheet of 9" x 12" white construction paper, with outlines of 1 face and 2 arms
1 cardboard tube, about 5" in length
½ sheet of 9" x 12" white construction paper
1 small piece of tagboard, with feet outline
markers and scissors
tape and glue

Class Preparations:

For each child, duplicate the face and arm patterns on white construction paper and the feet pattern on tagboard. Also cut a piece of 9" x 6" white construction paper.

Directions:

1. Cut the white construction paper to fit around the tube and glue to secure.
2. Color the face with markers to look like your Dad. Don't forget features such as glasses, a beard, or a moustache. Cut out the face.
3. Glue the face on the top of the tube and use markers to decorate the rest of the body. You could draw on things to show your Dad's favorite hobby, such as a baseball bat or a fishing rod.
4. Color the arms to match the body; then cut out and glue on.
5. Color and cut out the tagboard feet. Glue the tube to the feet to complete the pen holder.

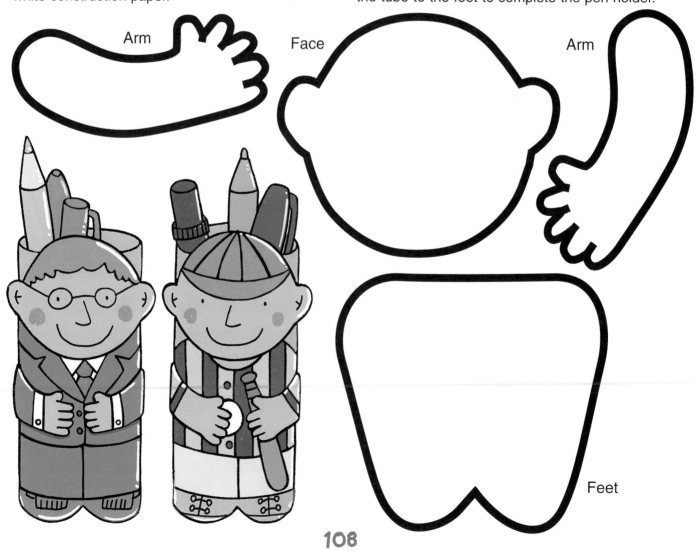

Arm

Face

Arm

Feet

Have your students look out for butterflies. Then use these projects to make a colorful class display.

spring

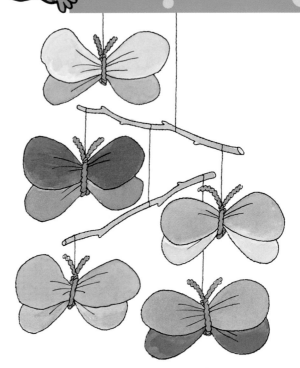

Oriental Butterfly Fan

Materials For Each Child:
1/4 sheet of 9" x 12" colored construction paper
tissue-paper scraps in assorted colors
2 craft sticks
colored markers, pencil, scissors, and glue

Class Preparations:
For each child, cut a 4 1/2" x 6" piece of colored construction paper.

Directions:
1. Cut around the corners of the construction paper to make a rounded rectangular fan.
2. Glue the craft sticks back to back on either side of the fan to sandwich the fan and make a handle, as shown. **H**
3. Fold a piece of tissue paper in half and carefully draw the shape of a butterfly wing against the fold. Cut out, but do not cut along the fold. Open out and glue on the fan.
4. Cut and glue on more tissue-paper shapes to pattern the butterfly's wings. Each time, fold a piece of tissue paper and cut out a shape to make two identical pieces. Then glue one piece to each wing, keeping the design symmetrical.
5. Cut a body from tissue paper and glue on. Finally, add antennae and eyes with colored markers.

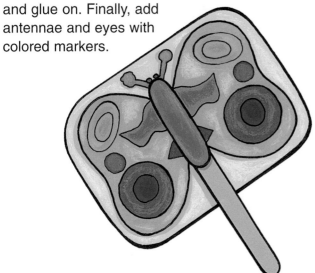

Fluttering Butterflies

Materials For Each Child:
2 pieces of different-colored tissue paper, 3" x 6"
1 pipe cleaner, about 6" in length
scissors

Class Preparations:
For this group project, have strong thread and several twigs ready to display the butterflies.

Directions:
1. Fold a pipe cleaner in half.
2. Lay one piece of tissue paper on top of the other. Cut around the corners to make ovals; then gather together the center.
3. Place the gathered part of the tissue paper in the bend in the pipe cleaner. Twist together the halves of the pipe cleaner to secure, and leave the ends sticking up to make antennae.
4. Separate the pieces of tissue paper to fluff out your butterfly wings.
5. Tie strong thread to the butterfly's body. Tie a butterfly to the end of each twig; then hang several twigs together to make a class mobile, as shown. **T**

Get your class in the mood for summer. Use sand, pebbles, and shells for seaside crafts and artwork.

Submarine View

Materials For Each Child:
2 paper plates, 7" in diameter
clear plastic wrap
yarn scraps, sand, pebbles, and shells
stapler to share
blue tempera paint and paintbrush
colored markers, pencil, scissors, and glue

Directions:
1. Cut out the center of one paper plate to leave a 1" rim (see Practical Tips, page 4). Put the center to one side. Use markers to color a porthole design on the underside of the rim.
2. Turn the rim over and spread glue around the edge. Stretch wrap across to make a porthole window. Allow to dry; then trim the plastic wrap.
3. Paint the second plate blue. Allow to dry.
4. Draw several fish shapes on the center section of the first plate. Color and cut out.
5. Glue the fish to the center of the second plate. Add sand, pebbles, shells, and yarn to make an underwater scene; then allow to dry.
6. Place the porthole window on top of the second plate. Staple all around the edge to finish your submarine view. 🄗

Footprints In The Sand

Materials For Each Child:
2 sheets of 9" x 12" yellow construction paper
tissue-paper scraps in 2 or more shades of blue
sand
pencil
scissors
glue

Directions:
1. Take off your shoes and socks. Stand on a sheet of yellow construction paper and have a friend draw around your feet. Cut out the shapes.
2. Spread glue on the footprints and sprinkle on sand. Allow to dry; then pour off the excess.
3. Glue the footprints to a second sheet of yellow construction paper.
4. Tear strips of blue tissue paper and glue along one long edge of the paper to make a shoreline, as shown. Allow to dry.

Ship At Sea

Materials For Each Child:

2 sheets of 9" x 12" white tagboard, with outlines
   of several waves, 1 ship, and 2 seagulls
1 shoe box
2 or 3 bottle tops
tempera paints in bright colors and paintbrushes
colored markers and scissors
string, thread, tape, and glue

Class Preparations:

Duplicate the patterns on this page and on page
112 on tagboard so that each child has outlines
of one ship, two seagulls, and several waves.

Directions:

1. Stand the shoe box with the opening facing
you. Cut a 1" vertical slit near the bottom of the
left-hand side of the box, about halfway back. ⓗ

2. Paint the top half of the inside of the box light
blue with white clouds for the sky. Paint the
bottom half dark blue for the sea. Paint bright
stripes on the outside of the box. Allow to dry.

3. Cut out several waves. Fold each wave along
the dotted line to make a flap; then paint the
section above the flap dark blue. Allow to dry.

4. Make two long waves by gluing waves end to
end and trimming as necessary to fit inside your
shoe box. Spread glue on the flap of one wave;
then stick it near the back of the box. ⓗ

5. Color and cut out the two seagulls. Tape a
piece of thread to each and tape the other end
inside the top of the box.

6. Color and cut out the ship. Glue on string
for ropes and bottle tops for portholes.

7. Cut a tagboard strip, 3/4" wide and slightly
longer than your box. Push one end through
the slit in your box. Glue the ship to this.

8. Glue the second strip of waves to the
front of the box. Allow to dry; then push
and pull the tagboard strip to move the
ship across the sea. ⓗ

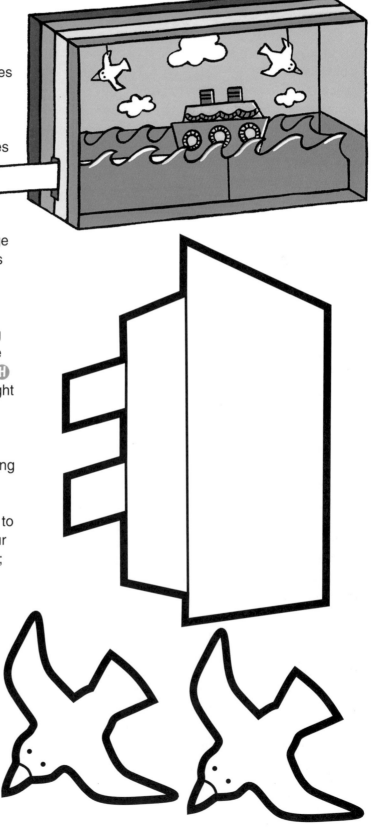

111

Use with Ship At Sea on page 111.

Seaside Print

. . . .

Materials For Each Child:
1 cookie sheet
1 piece of white construction paper,
  about the same size as the cookie sheet
1 craft stick
fabric rags to share
drawing paper
green or blue tempera paint, mixed with
  a little flour, glue, and liquid detergent
thick paintbrush and pencil

Class Preparations:
Mix tempera paint with a little flour, glue,
and liquid detergent to a thick consistency.

Directions:
1. Practice drawing a simple sea picture
on drawing paper.
2. Use a paintbrush to cover the cookie sheet
with a thin layer of paint.
3. Use a craft stick to quickly scrape the
outlines of your picture in the paint. Use
long strokes.
4. Carefully lay the construction paper on top
of the paint. Rub the back gently with a rag. Try
not to move the paper or the picture will blur.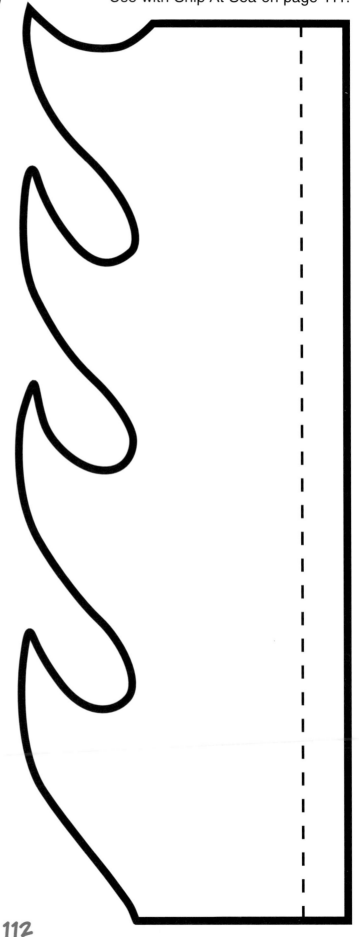
5. Slowly peel off the paper to reveal
your print.

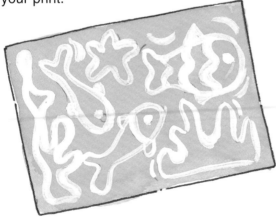

Woolly Octopus

Materials For Each Child:
1 square of thick cardboard, 8" x 8"
1 ball of thick knitting yarn, about 120'
1 long piece of elastic
2 wiggle eyes
scissors and glue

Class Preparations:
Cut a square of cardboard for each child.

Directions:
1. Cut ten short pieces of yarn. Wind the rest of the yarn around the cardboard about 80 times. Cut through the yarn at one end and remove the card, keeping the yarn looped double.
2. Tie a short piece of yarn around the bundle, about 1" below the loops. Tie another piece about 2" below this to make a head (A). Cut through the loops at the top. 🌀
3. Divide the yarn below the head into eight sections. Braid each one to make a tentacle. Tie a piece of yarn around the end of each tentacle. 🌀
4. Glue wiggle eyes on the head.
5. Tie on elastic for hanging your octopus. 🌀

Tropical Fish

Materials For Each Child:
1 sheet of 9" x 12" pale blue construction paper
drinking straw
tempera paints in blue, green, red, orange, yellow, turquoise, and black
paintbrushes

Class Preparations:
Provide pictures of tropical puffer fish for the children to look at.

Directions:
1. Use a paintbrush to drip a large pool of paint on the paper.
2. Position the end of the straw close to the paint and blow. Try to blow lines of paint at different angles to resemble a tropical puffer fish.
3. Repeat with different colors of paint to make more fish; then allow to dry.
4. Use a paintbrush to add eyes, fins, and a tail to each fish.

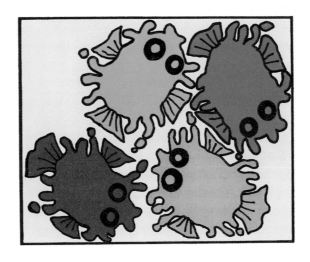

Terrific Turtle

Materials For Each Child:

1 sheet of 9" x 12" white construction paper
4 sheets of white drawing paper
a set of 4 turtle templates, to share
4 different materials for rubbing, such as fabric, lace, sandpaper, and corrugated cardboard
4 different-colored crayons
blue tempera paint and sponge
black marker, pencil, scissors, and glue

Class Preparations:

Use the patterns on the opposite page to make sets of four templates for the children to share.

Directions:

1. Dip a sponge in blue paint and print all over the white construction paper. Allow to dry.
2. Place a piece of drawing paper on top of a textured surface and rub over it with a crayon.
3. Use different materials and different-colored crayons to make three more rubbings.
4. Use a pencil to trace a different template on the back of each rubbing and cut out. Glue the pieces together to make a multi-colored turtle. ⓗ
5. Add eyes with a marker and glue your turtle on the blue background.

Crab Legs

Materials For Each Child:

1 paper plate, 7" in diameter
8 strips of orange construction paper, 1½" x 6"
2 wiggle eyes
orange tempera paint and paintbrush
scissors and glue

Class Preparations:

For each child, cut eight strips of orange construction paper, measuring 1½" x 6".

Directions:

1. Paint the underside of the plate orange.
2. Fold a strip of paper in half lengthwise; then cut around one corner, as shown (A), to make a leg. ⓗ
3. Make two cuts in the leg, as shown (A). Cut towards the fold but do not cut right through; then bend the leg to make two joints (B). ⓗ
4. Repeat steps 2 and 3 to make seven more legs.
5. Glue the legs around the unpainted side of the plate, facing forward. Finally, glue on wiggle eyes.

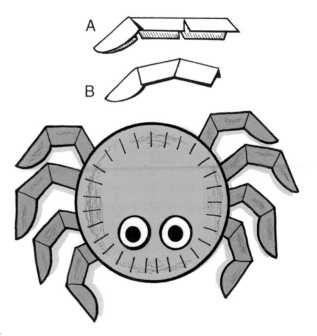

Use with Terrific Turtle
on page 114.

1   2   3   4

Handy Fish Puppet

Materials For Each Child:
½ sheet of 9" x 12" white
   construction paper
brightly colored paper scraps
1 wiggle eye
1 craft stick
scissors and pencil
tape and glue

Class Preparations:
Show the children pictures of tropical fish.
Then, have the children tear paper scraps
into quarter-size pieces. Sort colors into
several boxes for the children to share. Cut
sheets of white construction paper in halves.

Directions:
1. Trace around your hand on construction
paper and cut out the shape.
2. Glue on colored paper scraps to make
tropical fish patterns.
3. Cut a strip of paper for a mouth and glue
it on the fish; then glue on a wiggle eye.
4. Tape a craft stick to the back of the
fish to make a handle for your puppet.

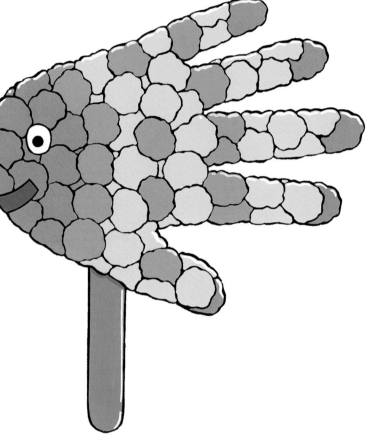

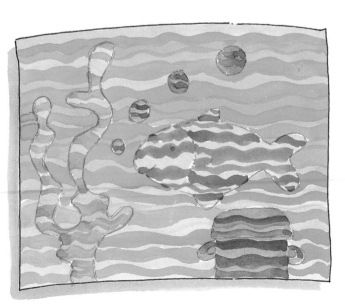

Underwater Pictures

Materials For Each Child:
1 sheet of 9" x 12" white construction paper
colored markers
pencil

Directions:
1. Use a pencil to draw an underwater scene
lightly on a sheet of construction paper. You
could include seaweed, fish, a treasure chest,
or a shipwreck, but keep the picture simple.
2. Color the picture by drawing lines across the
page, changing color wherever necessary. Do
not use a ruler to draw the lines. Wavy freehand
lines will give the scene an underwater feel.

Memorial Day is an ideal time to explore great American achievements, such as the first moon landing.

Patriotic Pencil Holder

Materials For Each Child:
1 strip of white construction paper, 2" x 6"
2 pencils
self-hardening modeling clay, the size of
   a tennis ball
tempera paint and paintbrush
old toothbrush, to share
red and blue markers
glue

Directions:
1. Fold the strip of paper in half widthwise and color a "Stars and Stripes" flag on each side.
2. Unfold the paper and spread glue on the plain side. Wrap the flag around the blunt end of a pencil and press the two sides firmly together.
3. Mold the modeling clay into a half-ball shape. Use the blunt end of another pencil to make two or three holes in the clay. Wiggle the pencil to widen the holes slightly; then pull it out.
4. Use an old toothbrush to roughen the surface of the clay. Allow to harden.
5. Paint the clay to look like the surface of the moon.
6. Display your pencil flag in your patriotic pencil holder.

Fireworks Display

Materials For Each Child:
1 coffee filter
various diluted food colorings
   in shallow containers
eye drop dispensers, to share
scissors and glue

Class Preparations:
For this group project, mix different food colorings with a little water. Fix several sheets of black construction paper to the classroom wall, ready to display the children's fireworks.

Directions:
1. Fold a filter paper in half, in half again, then in half again.
2. Dip each corner of the folded filter paper in a different container of food coloring.
3. Use an eye drop dispenser to add drops of food coloring in the center. Unfold the filter paper and allow to dry.
4. Cut a fringe, 2" deep, all around the edge of the filter paper. **H**
5. Glue all the filter papers to the black wall display. Gently raise the fringe to resemble an exploding firework. **T**

Windmills

• • • • • • • • • • • • •

Materials For Each Child:
1 square of black construction paper, 7" x 7"
4 brightly colored crepe-paper streamers
1 long pin
1 paper straw
small amount of modeling clay
red, yellow, and green tempera paints
   in squeeze bottles
paintbrush
scissors, tape, and glue

Directions:
1. Make circles of paint on the paper, about
1" apart, by squeezing the paint from
the bottle (A).
2. Pull the blunt end of a paintbrush through the
paint from the center of the paper to the edge.
Repeat several times around the circle (B).
Allow to dry.

3. Turn over the paper and cut a 4" slit from
each corner of the square towards the center,
as shown (C). 🅗
4. Dab on glue as shown (C), then bend
the glued point toward the center (D) and
press firmly. Allow to dry. 🅗
5. Push a pin through the center of the
windmill, passing through all four glued points.
Turn the windmill over; then push the pin through
the tip of a straw into a small ball of modeling
clay to secure. 🅗
6. Tape a paper streamer to each corner of your
windmill and watch it whizz around in the wind.

A

B

C
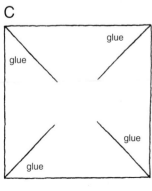

D
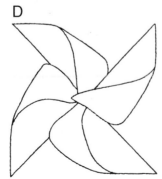

anytime

Weather Wheel

Materials For Each Child:
½ sheet of 9" x 12" blue construction paper
¼ sheet of 9" x 12" white construction paper
1 small and 1 large circle template, to share
brass fastener and colored crayons
black marker, pencil, scissors, and ruler

Class Preparations:
Use the patterns on the opposite page
to make large and small tagboard circle
templates for the children to share.

Directions:
1. Use the templates to trace a large circle
on blue construction paper and a small circle
on white construction paper; then cut out.
2. Draw an arrow on the small circle and
write "Today's weather".
3. Use a pencil and ruler to divide the larger
circle into six sections. Ⓗ
4. Place the small circle on top of the larger
one and join in the center with a brass fastener.
5. In each section of the outer circle, draw a
picture to illustrate a type of weather. Write the
name of each type of weather beneath. Every
day, point the arrow to the right weather picture.

Rainbow Collage

Materials For Each Child:
1 sheet of 12" x 18" construction paper
old magazines
cotton batting
pencil, scissors, and glue

Directions:
1. Draw a rainbow outline across the paper.
Divide the rainbow into seven stripes and label
each stripe with a rainbow color: red, orange,
yellow, green, blue, indigo, and violet. Ⓗ
2. Tear or cut scraps of each rainbow color
from old magazines; then glue the scraps
on the right section of the rainbow.
3. Cut out the rainbow.
4. Cut a fluffy cloud from cotton batting
and glue it on the end of your rainbow.

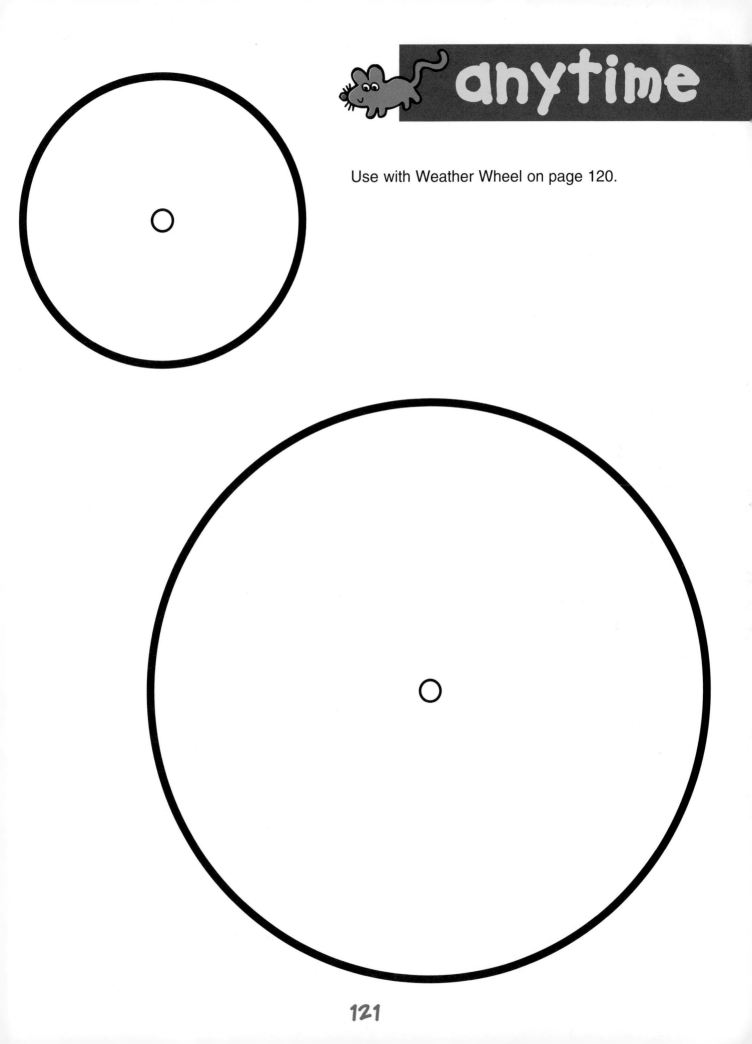

anytime

Use with Weather Wheel on page 120.

Learn about different cultures with these Mexican and Native American decorations.

Mexican Wall Hanging

Materials For Each Child:
1 circular aluminum-foil dish
1 piece of string, 6" in length
a ball-point pen
sharp pencil

Directions:
1. Turn the dish upside-down. Use a ball-point pen to trace a zigzag design around the edge.
2. Draw a sun face in the center of the dish.
3. Use a sharp pencil to make a hole in the top of the dish (see Practical Tips, page 4). Thread string through the hole and tie in a loop. Ⓗ
4. Turn the dish over so that your design stands out from the surface of the dish; then hang it up. Ⓗ

Totem Pole

Materials For Each Child:
2 sheets of 9" x 12" tagboard,
    with 4 wing outlines
4 cardboard cartons in different sizes
collage materials such as plastic cutlery,
    paper cups and plates, small containers,
    plastic lids, yarn, wiggle eyes, and corks
tempera paints and paintbrushes
pencil, scissors, and glue

Class Preparations:
Enlarge and duplicate the wing pattern on the opposite page on tagboard four times for each child.

Directions:
1. Cut out the tagboard wings. Glue wings to two of the cartons, as shown.
2. Decorate the boxes and wings with paints. Allow to dry.
3. Glue collage materials on each box to make faces.
4. Stack the boxes to make a totem pole.

Papel Picado

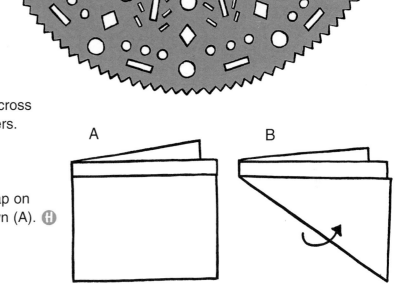

Materials For Each Child:

1 piece of brightly colored
  tissue paper, about 12" x 7"
pinking shears (optional)
scissors and glue

Class Preparations:

For each child, cut a piece of tissue paper
about 12" x 7". Tie a long piece of string across
your classroom to display the paper banners.

Directions:

1. Fold over one of the long edges of the
tissue paper to make a 1" flap. With the flap on
the outside, fold the paper in half, as shown (A). Ⓗ
2. Fold the bottom left-hand corner of
the paper up to the flap, as shown (B).
Fold again twice more. Ⓗ
3. Use pinking shears or scissors to cut
zigzags in the right-hand end.
4. Cut out shapes from the folded edge,
as shown (C). Unfold once and cut more
shapes. Unfold again and cut again.
5. Unfold the paper completely. Spread
glue inside the flap and hang on the string. Ⓗ

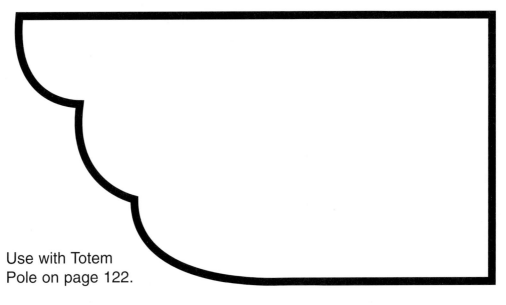

Use with Totem
Pole on page 122.

123

Navajo Sun Medallion

Materials For Each Child:
1 piece of cardboard, at least 10" x 10"
1 paper plate, 10" in diameter
1 sun template
tempera paints, sand, and glue mixed in
   plastic containers
paintbrushes
plastic fork, pencil, and scissors

Class Preparations:
Use the pattern on the opposite page
to make a template for each child. Mix two
parts sand with one part glue and one part
tempera paint in plastic containers to make
thick, gritty paint in several colors.

Directions:
1. Trace around a paper plate on a
piece of cardboard and cut out the circle.
2. Use the template to trace a sun
on the circle; then draw on a face.
3. Use the thick paint mixtures to
carefully paint your picture.
4. Scrape designs in the paint with
a plastic fork while the paint is still wet.

Gift Of Stationery

Materials For Each Child:
several sheets of writing paper
   and several envelopes
1 piece of narrow ribbon, 20" in length
different-shaped printing tools, to share
tempera paints in shallow dishes

Class Preparations:
Cut circles, triangles, and squares from
posterboard. Glue each shape to the blunt
end of a pencil to make printing tools for
the children to share.

Directions:
1. Dip a printing tool in paint and print a design
around the edge of each sheet of paper. Print
the front of each envelope in the same way.
2. Allow to dry; then print on the back of
each envelope, if desired.
3. Gather the paper and envelopes into
a bundle and tie with a ribbon. ⊕

Use with Navajo Sun Medallion on page 124.

Why not let the children choose which clock they would like to make? Then display all the clocks together.

Friendly Clock

Materials For Each Child:

$1/2$ sheet of 9" x 12" white construction paper, with outlines of a clock face, hands, eyes, mouth, and feet

1 sheet of 9" x 12" colored construction paper

1 empty individual-size cereal carton

construction-paper scraps

a brass fastener

colored markers, scissors, and glue

Class Preparations:

For each child, duplicate the clock face, hands, eyes, mouth, and feet patterns below on white construction paper.

Directions:

1. Cut a piece of colored construction paper to fit around the carton and glue in place.

2. Color and cut out the clock face and hands; then glue the clock face on the carton.

3. Push a brass fastener through the hands and through the center of the clock face. Ⓗ

4. Color and cut out the eyes, mouth, and feet. Glue them on the carton and draw on rosy cheeks. Glue on paper scraps for hair.

Use with Friendly Clock on this page, Haunted House Clock on page 127, and Rocket Clock on page 128.

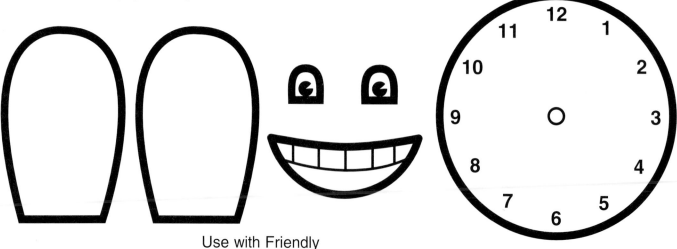

Use with Friendly Clock on this page.

Ask your students to set their clocks to a specific time, such as the time they get up or breaktime.

Haunted House Clock

Materials For Each Child:
1 sheet of 9" x 12" white construction paper, with
  outlines of a clock face, hands, and 2 turrets
1 sheet of 9" x 12" colored construction paper
1 construction-paper semicircle, 7" in diameter
1 empty individual-size cereal carton
a brass fastener
colored markers, scissors, and glue

Class Preparations:
For each child, duplicate the clock face and hands on the opposite page and the turrets below on construction paper. Use a 7" paper plate to trace and cut out construction-paper circles. Cut in half and give each child a semicircle.

Directions:
1. Color the semicircle; then fold it to make a cone for a roof and glue to secure. Allow to dry. Ⓗ
2. Follow steps 1–3 for Friendly Clock (opposite).
3. Decorate the house with markers. Draw on a door, windows, spiders, and ghosts.
4. Color the turrets; then fold them along the dotted lines and spread glue on the flaps. Glue the turrets and roof on the house.

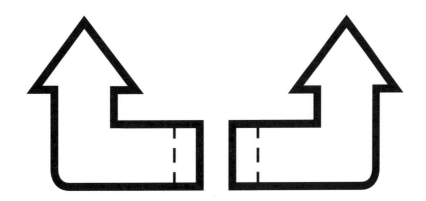

Rocket Clock

Materials For Each Child:
¼ sheet of 9" x 12" white construction paper,
  with outlines of a clock face and hands
¼ sheet of 9" x 12" blue tagboard,
  with 2 wing outlines
1 sheet of 9" x 12" gray construction paper
1 construction-paper semicircle, 7" in diameter
1 empty drink can
a brass fastener
colored markers, scissors, and glue

Class Preparations:
For each child, duplicate the clock face and
hands on page 126 on white construction paper.
Duplicate the wing patterns on this page on blue
tagboard. Use a 7" paper plate to trace and cut
out construction-paper circles. Cut in half and
give each child a semicircle.

Directions:
1. Fold the semicircle to make a cone for the
rocket nose and glue to secure. Allow to dry. ⓗ
2. Glue the gray paper around the can, so
that it sticks up above the top.
3. Color and cut out the clock face and hands.
Glue the clock face to the top of the rocket
(above the can).
4. Push a brass fastener through the hands
and through the center of the clock face. ⓗ
5. Use markers to decorate the rocket.
6. Draw rivets on the wings and cut them out.
Fold each wing along the dotted line to make a
flap. Spread glue on the flaps and
glue a wing to each side of the rocket.
7. Glue the nose on top of the rocket.

Shell Frame

Materials For Each Child:

1 large piece of non-hardening
   modeling clay
1 posterboard square, about 6" x 6"
a drawing or photo, about 4" square
a variety of shells, to share
plaster of Paris
tempera paints, paintbrushes, ruler, and glue

Class Preparations:

Have children collect shells. Prepare plaster of
Paris according to the instructions on the packet.
Mix equal parts of glue and water.

Directions:

1. Mold modeling clay into a square shape about
7" x 7" and 2" thick. Flatten the edges with a ruler
to make a square. Press a trough all around the
square to make a mold, as shown (A). 🅗

2. Make shell prints in the clay mold by pressing
in shells and pulling them out.

3. Pour plaster into the mold. Allow to harden.

4. Peel away the clay from the plaster.

5. Paint the raised shell prints and background.

6. Allow to dry; then paint watered-down glue
all over the frame. Glue around the edge of the
picture and attach to the back of the frame.

7. Cut a triangle from posterboard. Fold a flap
along one edge and glue to the back of the
frame (see instructions on page 20). When dry,
stand up your frame. 🅗

Cartoon Pot

Materials For Each Child:

1 terracotta flowerpot
colorful cartoons from old magazines,
   comics, newspapers, and greetings cards
paintbrush, scissors, and glue

Directions:

1. Cut out lots of cartoon characters and
speech bubbles from old comics and magazines.

2. Glue on the cutouts to cover the outside of
the pot. Allow to dry.

3. Brush glue all over the pot to varnish it.
Allow to dry; then add another coat of glue.

Monkey Chain

• • • • • • • • • • • • • • • • • • • •

Materials For Each Child:
4 sheets of 9" x 12" construction paper
 in various colors
1 monkey template
colored markers, pencil, and scissors

Class Preparations:
Use the pattern on the opposite page to make
a template for each child.

Directions:

1. Use the template to trace and cut out
a monkey from construction paper.
2. Draw and color a face with markers.
3. Use different colors of paper to make three
more monkeys.
4. Hook the monkeys together by their arms
and tails and hang the top one from a shelf
or from your desk. **H**

Toadstool Pin

• • • • • • • • • • • • • • • • • • • •

Materials For Each Child:
self-hardening modeling clay
blunt knife
fabric scrap
safety pin, scissors, and glue
brown, red, and white tempera paints
paintbrushes

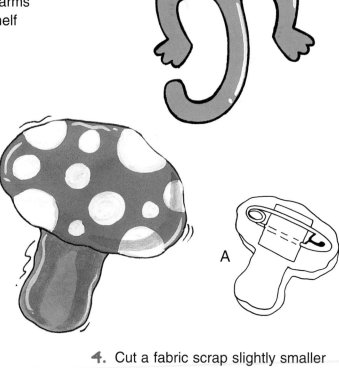

A

Directions:

1. Use your hand to flatten the clay
on the table so that it is about 3/4" thick.
Cut out a rough toadstool shape with a blunt
knife. Mold the clay to neaten the shape. **H**
2. Allow to harden overnight.
3. Paint the toadstool stalk brown and
the top red with white spots. Allow to dry.

4. Cut a fabric scrap slightly smaller
than the top of the toadstool. Soak it in glue,
then use it to attach a safety pin to the back
of the toadstool, as shown (A). **H**
5. Brush glue all over the toadstool
as a varnish, then allow to dry.

130

Tell your students about different animals from around the world. Here are lots of ideas to get you started!

Use with Monkey Chain on page 130.

Circus Elephants

Materials For Each Child:
1 sheet of 9" x 12" light gray tagboard
1/4 sheet of 9" x 12" light gray construction paper,
  with 2 ear outlines
1 elephant template, to share
drawing-paper scraps
colored construction-paper scraps
yarn and sequins
gray tempera paint in a shallow container
colored markers, pencil, scissors, and glue

Class Preparations:
Use the pattern on the right to make elephant templates for the children to share. Duplicate the ear pattern on the opposite page twice for each child.

Directions:
1. Fold the tagboard in half. Trace the elephant template with the dotted line along the fold. Cut it out, but do not cut along the fold.
2. Cut out the ears. Turn one ear over to face the opposite way. Crumple a piece of drawing paper and dip it into the gray paint. Dab all over the ears and the elephant to make a textured effect. Allow to dry.
3. Cut a rectangle from colored paper and glue over the elephant's back to make a blanket.
4. Fold along the dotted lines on the ears to make flaps. Spread glue on the flaps and glue one ear on each side of the elephant.
5. Tie a knot in the end of a piece of yarn and glue on the back of the elephant.

6. Glue on sequins to decorate the elephant's blanket. Use a marker to draw eyes and toes.
7. Arrange the class elephants in a long line with each yarn tail touching the next elephant's trunk to make a parade of circus elephants. Ⓣ

Use with Circus
Elephants on
page 132.

fold

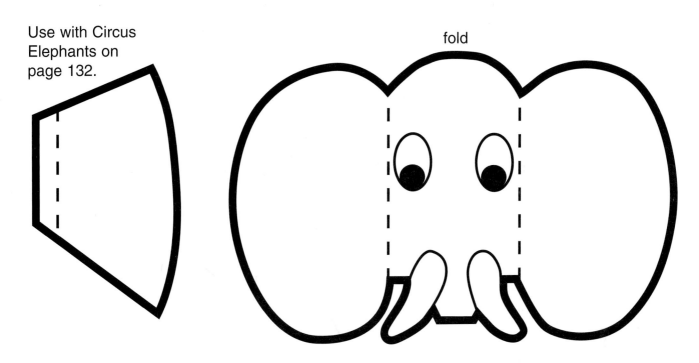

Jumbo
Elephant Straw

Materials For Each Child:
¹⁄₄ sheet of 9" x 12" gray construction paper,
   with elephant head outline
drinking straw
colored markers, scissors, and tape

Class Preparations:
For each child, duplicate the elephant
head pattern above on gray construction paper.

Directions:
1. Use markers to decorate the elephant's
ears with spots and swirls.
2. Cut out the elephant's head.
3. Fold the elephant's head in half, so that the
decorated side shows. Fold the ears forward
along the dotted lines. Open it out a little,
so that it is bent slightly along the folds.
4. Tape a drinking straw to the back of
the elephant's head to make a trunk.

Wiggly Snake

• • • • • • • • • • • • • • • • • • • •

Materials For Each Child:

8 paper cups
14 brass fasteners
1 long piece of string
colored markers and pencil

Directions:

1. Use colored markers to decorate the sides of the cups with matching zigzag patterns.
2. Use a pencil to make a hole in the bottom of one cup (see Practical Tips, page 4). Tie a knot at the end of a piece of string and thread the string through the hole from inside the cup. Also, make two holes in opposite sides of the cup near the top (A). 🄷
3. Make four holes in each of the other seven cups, two opposite each other near the bottom and two opposite each other near the top (B).
4. Starting with the cup with string attached, push fasteners through the holes to attach the cups in a line, as shown. 🄷
5. Use a marker to draw eyes on the first cup.

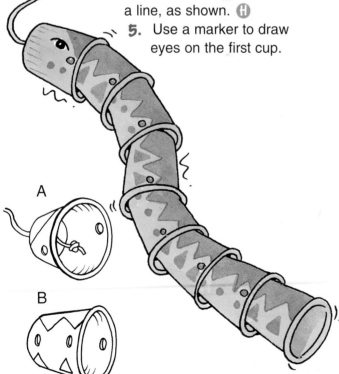

A

B

Tall Giraffe Mural

• •

Materials For Group Project:

1 piece of yellow bulletin-board paper, with giraffe outline
1 piece of white bulletin-board paper
1 wiggle eye
bark pieces or wood chips
pieces of foam packing material
tempera paints and paintbrushes
scissors and glue

Class Preparations:

For this group project, enlarge the pattern on the opposite page on yellow bulletin-board paper. Collect bark pieces or wood chips. Provide pictures of a giraffe's skin patterns and surroundings, and have a hot-glue gun ready.

Directions:

1. Paint the white bulletin-board paper to look like an African plain. Allow to dry.
2. Cut out the giraffe.
3. Break bark or wood chips into small pieces.
4. Hot-glue the bark or wood chips to the giraffe to make a pattern. 🅣
5. Glue on a wiggle eye.
6. Turn over the giraffe and glue pieces of foam on it. Allow to dry. Spread glue on the foam pieces; then fix the giraffe to the background.

Use with Tall Giraffe Mural
on page 134.

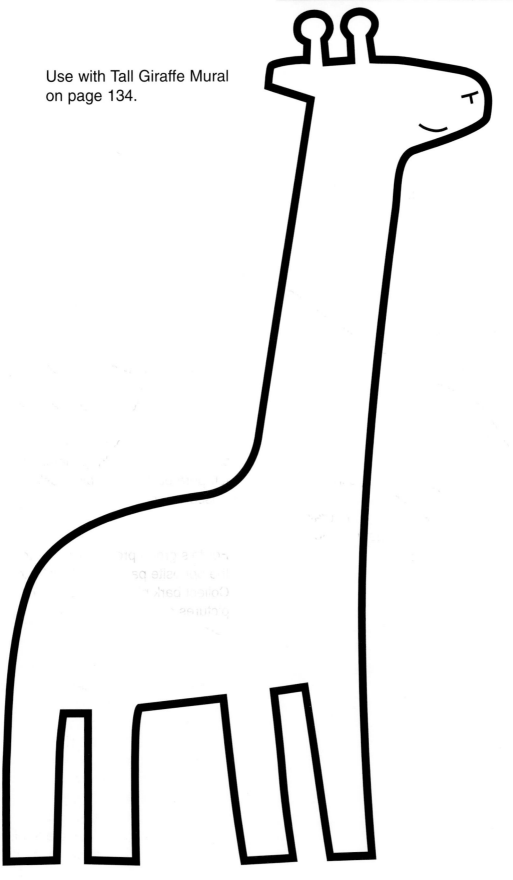

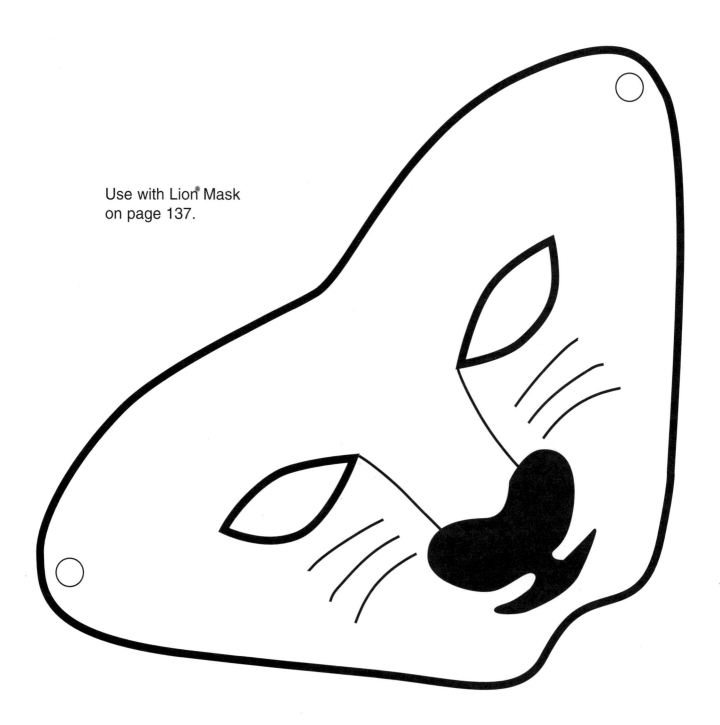

Use with Lion Mask
on page 137.

Snazzy Snake

Materials For Each Child:
1 sheet of 9" x 12" tagboard
1 paper plate, 7" in diameter
selection of small objects for printing, such as
   bottle lids, corks, and carrot and celery slices
red construction-paper scrap and scissors
needle and thread
pencil
tempera paints in shallow containers
paintbrush

Directions:
1. Trace around a paper plate on tagboard and cut out the circle.
2. Use a pencil to draw a spiral from the outside of the circle to the center. Leave a circle in the center for the snake's head. 🖐
3. Dip small objects in paint and use them to print a colorful repeated design along the snake's body. Use a brush to paint on eyes. Allow to dry.
4. Cut along the pencil line. Cut out a tongue from red paper and glue it on the head.
5. Thread the needle and knot the thread. Push the needle through the snake's head. 🖐
6. Hang up the snake and gently pull the body down to form a spiral which will twist and turn. 🖐

Lion Mask

Materials For Each Child:
1 sheet of 9" x 12" yellow construction paper, with mask outline
1 long piece of elastic thread
yellow and light brown tissue paper
glitter and black marker
scissors and glue

Class Preparations:
Duplicate the pattern on the opposite page on yellow construction paper for each child.

Directions:
1. Cut around the mask. Cut out the eyes and use a pencil to make a hole in each side, where marked (see Practical Tips, page 4).
2. Thread elastic through one of the holes at the side and tie. Hold the mask in place on your face and have a friend thread the elastic through the other hole and tie it tight. Trim the end. 🖐
3. Tear tissue paper into narrow triangles, 3" in length. Glue the tissue paper around the edge of the mask, pointing outward. Glue more rows inside the first pieces, as shown.
4. Dot glue on the mask and sprinkle on glitter.

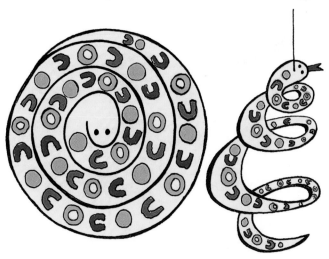

anytime

Patchwork Spiders

Materials For Each Child:
4 sheets of 9" x 12" white construction paper
1 octagon template and 1 square template
colored markers
pencil
scissors
glue

Class Preparations:
Use the patterns below to make octagon and square templates from tagboard for each child.

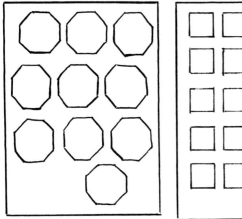

Directions:
1. Use markers to color three sheets of paper. Use a different pattern and different colors for each sheet.
2. Use a template to trace about 20 octagons on the back of two of the sheets; then cut out. Use the other template to trace and cut out 20 squares from the third sheet.
3. Arrange the shapes on the sheet of white paper so that they fit together. First, lay down a row of one color of octagons alternating with squares. For the next row, use different-colored octagons and more squares. When you have covered the paper, glue the pieces in place and color in any gaps around the edges. Ⓗ
4. If desired, choose one color of octagon to be the spiders' bodies and draw two eyes and a smile on each body, as shown. Draw eight spider's legs around each body.

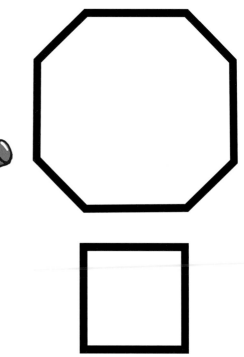

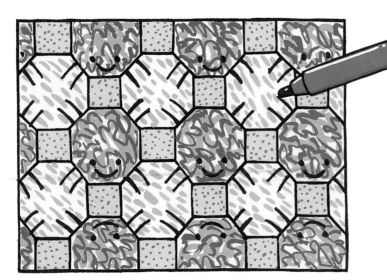

Owl Eyes

• • • • • • • • • • • • • •

Materials For Each Child:
1/2 sheet of 9" x 12" yellow construction paper,
   with owl eyes outline
1/2 sheet of 9" x 12" brown construction paper
2 pipe cleaners
black marker
pencil
scissors and tape
glue

Class Preparations:
For each child, duplicate the pattern on this page
on yellow construction paper and cut a 4 1/2" x 12"
piece of brown construction paper.

Directions:
1. Cut around the owl eyes pattern and cut
out the eye holes (see Practical Tips, page 4).
2. Draw around the eye holes with a
black marker.
3. Accordion-fold the brown paper. Draw feather
shapes, about 2" in length, on the top layer. Cut
out through all the layers to make lots of feathers
at once. Snip around the edge of each feather
to make a fringe.
4. Glue the feathers
on the back of the
owl eyes.
5. Bend both ends of a
pipe cleaner and tape
one end to the owl
eyes. Repeat with
another pipe
cleaner on the
other side.
6. Wear your
glasses like a
wise old owl!

139

Find out which books the children like to read at home and let them recommend them to other classmates.

Wise Owl Bookmark

Materials For Each Child:
1/4 sheet of 9" x 12" brown construction paper, with owl and wing outlines
1/6 sheet of 9" x 12" white construction paper
yellow and white gummed dots
colored markers
scissors
pencil and ruler
glue

Class Preparations:
For each child, duplicate the patterns below on brown construction paper and cut a strip of white construction paper, 9" x 2".

Directions:
1. Cut out the owl body and wing.
2. Decorate the owl and wing with colored markers. Use gummed dots for eyes.
3. Glue the owl's body to the top of the white paper strip. Spread glue near the top of the wing and glue it to the body. Allow to dry. **H**
4. Use the owl to mark your place in a book. Tuck the bottom of the wing over a page, as shown.

Flying Robin

Materials For Each Child:
1/4 sheet of 9" x 12" light brown
   construction paper, with
   robin outline
red construction-paper scrap
yellow construction-paper scrap
1 strip of tagboard, 1" x 7"
black marker
scissors
glue
tape or map pin

Class Preparations:
For each child, duplicate the pattern on this page on light brown construction paper and cut a strip of tagboard, measuring 1" x 7".

Directions:
1. Cut out the robin and cut a circle of red paper for the robin's breast.

2. Glue the red breast on the robin.
3. Use a black marker to add eyes and a beak to the robin and to color its legs.
4. Glue one end of the tagboard strip to the robin. Use tape or a map pin to attach the other end to the bulletin board. ⓗ

Texture Tortoise

· ·

Materials For Each Child:
1/2 sheet of 9" x 12" cream construction paper
1/2 sheet of 9" x 12" brown construction paper
1 set of tortoise templates, to share
variety of materials with different textures,
    such as corrugated cardboard,
    lunch bags, newspaper, felt, fabric,
    fur, cellophane, and tissue paper
black marker
pencil, scissors, and glue

Class Preparations:
Use the patterns on the opposite page to
make templates for the children to share.

Directions:
1. Use the templates to trace the tortoise
shell on cream construction paper and the
head and four legs on brown construction
paper; then cut out.
2. Glue the head and the legs on the
back of the shell, as shown.
3. Tear or cut a selection of different
materials into small pieces. Arrange them
on the front of the shell and glue in place.
4. Use a marker to add an eye and a mouth.

White Mouse Pin

· ·

Materials For Each Child:
1 cardboard scrap
1 large bottle top, to share
1 white cotton ball
2 small wiggle eyes
a safety pin
pink construction-paper scrap
pink felt scrap
a small black bead
pencil, scissors, tape, and glue

Directions:
1. Trace around a large bottle top on
cardboard and cut out the circle. Tape
a safety pin to the back of the circle. **(H)**
2. Glue the cotton ball to the front of
the circle to make a mouse.
3. Cut two ovals from pink construction
paper for ears and glue them on the mouse.
4. Cut a strip of pink felt for a tail and glue
to the back of the mouse.
5. Glue on wiggle eyes and a black
bead for a nose. Then wear your pet
mouse on your sweater!

Use with Texture Tortoise on page 142.

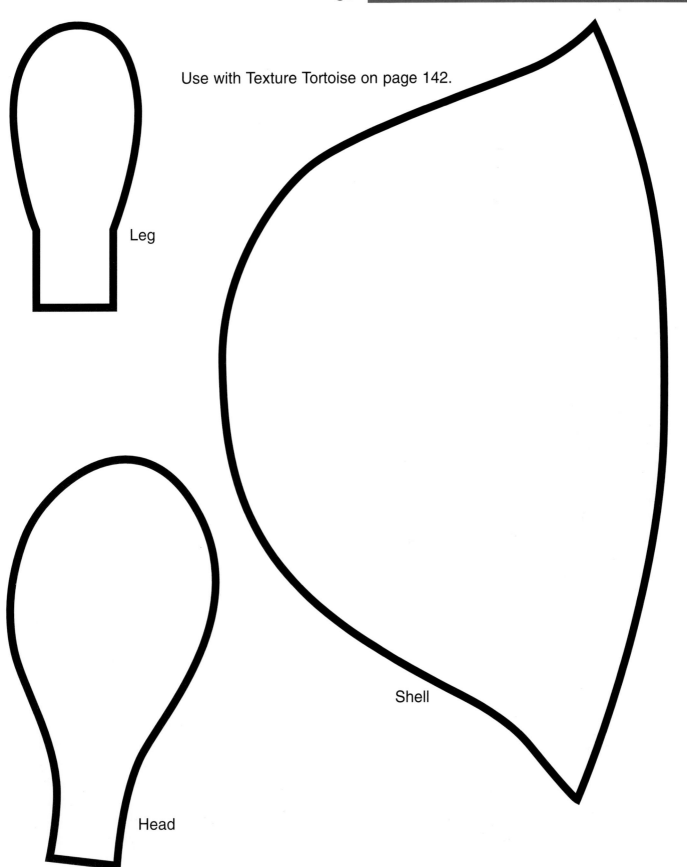

Leg

Shell

Head

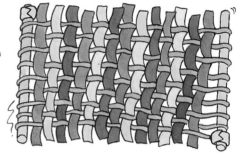

Dinosaurs are always a big favorite. Compare the size of a dinosaur with animals and buildings around today.

Box Loom Weaving

Materials For Each Child:
10 craft sticks
1 shoe box
a small ball of yarn
masking tape
a variety of fabric scraps and
  lengths of yarn
2 dowels, 6" in length

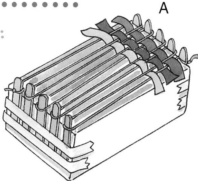

A

Directions:

1. Use masking tape to attach five craft sticks at regular intervals along one end of the box. Repeat at the opposite end.

2. Tie a long piece of yarn to the first stick at one end. Loop it around the opposite stick, pulling it taut, then loop it back and around the second stick. Continue until you reach the end. Tie the end of the yarn to the last stick. ⊕

3. Weave a strip of fabric or yarn under and over across the yarn on the loom. Take a different type of fabric or yarn and weave it first over, then under, as shown (A). Continue until the weaving is complete. ⊕

4. Slip each end of the weaving off the craft sticks and onto a dowel. Tape to secure. Hang the weaving on a nail or map pin. ⊕

Dinosaur Card

Materials For Each Child:
1 sheet of 9" x 12" dark green tagboard,
  with dinosaur outline
1/2 sheet of 9" x 12" light green construction
  paper
newspaper
watered-down yellow tempera paint and paintbrush
black marker
scissors and glue

Class Preparations:
For each child, duplicate the dinosaur pattern on the opposite page on dark green tagboard. Mix paint with water to a thin consistency.

Directions:

1. Cut out the dinosaur. Accordion-fold it along the dotted lines; then open it out.

2. Cut ovals from light green paper and glue them on the dinosaur's body.

3. Lay the dinosaur on newspaper; then use a brush to spatter yellow paint over it. Allow to dry.

4. Use a black marker to add an eye and toes.

5. Write a greeting on the back of the card, then fold it again to stand the dinosaur up.

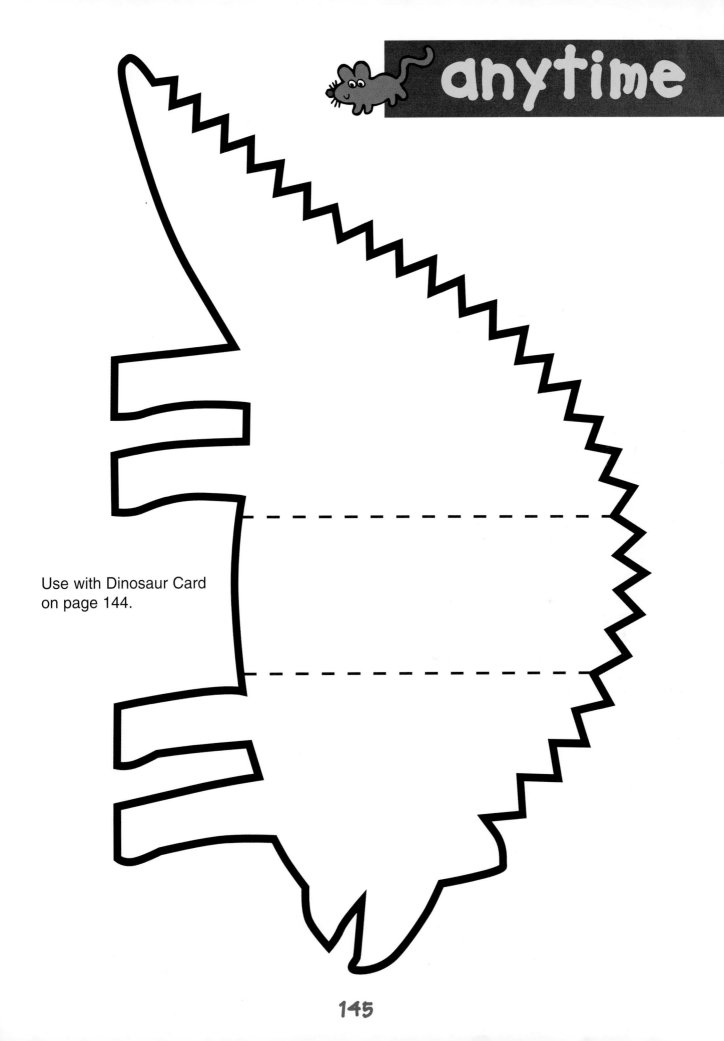

Use with Dinosaur Card
on page 144.

These projects will teach your youngsters about letters, numbers, and counting.

Money Saver

. . . .

Materials For Each Child:
1/2 sheet of 9" x 12" construction paper, with head and arms outline
1/4 sheet of 9" x 12" tagboard, with feet outline
1 rectangular, clear plastic food container with lid
colored construction-paper scraps
colored markers
scissors, tape, and glue

Class Preparations:
For each child, duplicate the head and arms pattern below on construction paper and the feet pattern on tagboard. Make a coin-sized slit in the lid of each container with a craft knife.

Directions:
1. Cut out the head and arms, and the feet.
2. Use markers to decorate the cutouts; then glue paper scraps on the head for hair.
3. Fold the head along the dotted line and tape the arms to one end of the container, as shown. Tape the feet to the other end. Tape the lid of the container to secure, if necessary.
4. Now post spare coins into your money saver through the slit.

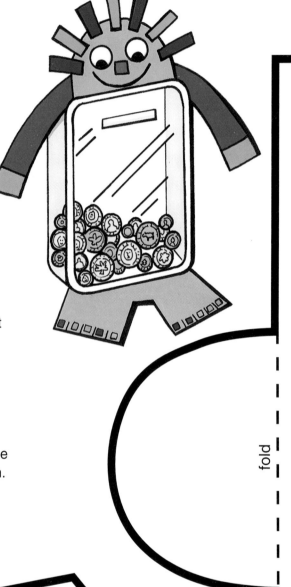

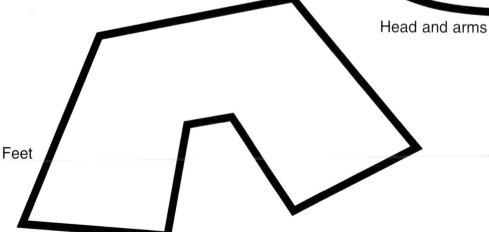

fold

Head and arms

Feet

Letter And Number Faces

. . . .

Materials For Each Child:
¹/₂ sheet of 9" x 12" construction paper
old magazines and newspapers
markers
scissors
glue

Directions:

1. Draw an oval for a face on construction paper.

2. Cut out large letters and numbers from magazines and newspapers.

3. Arrange the letters and numbers to make the features of a face and glue them in place on the paper.

Alphabet Doodling

. . . .

Materials For Each Child:
¹/₄ sheet of 9" x 12" construction paper
old magazines
colored markers
scissors and glue

Class Preparations:
For this group project, cut a 4¹/₂" x 6" piece of construction paper for each child and assign each child one letter of the alphabet. Have the whole class look in magazines for either upper or lower case letters, not a mixture. Have tape ready.

Directions:

1. Look through the magazines to find a large copy of your letter; then cut it out. If you cannot find a letter large enough, draw the outline of one on your paper.

2. Glue the letter in the center of the paper.

3. Doodle around the letter to turn it into a person or an animal. Look at the examples shown to help you.

4. Tape the class letters together in alphabetical order and tape to the wall. ⓣ

Salt-Dough Dominoes

Materials For Four Students:
2 quantities of salt dough
rolling pin, to share
blunt knife and ruler
cookie sheet
tempera paints in shallow containers
paintbrushes, pencil, and glue

Class Preparations:
Have children work in groups of four, each group making a set of 28 dominoes. Mix the salt dough according to the instructions on page 5. Make double the quantities for each group. You will need an oven to bake the dominoes.

Directions:
1. Roll out the dough to about 1/2" thick. Use a ruler and a blunt knife to cut out 28 dominoes, each measuring 1" x 2". Press the ruler across the center of each domino to make a line, as shown (A). 🅗
2. Place the dominoes on a cookie sheet and bake at 300°F for about an hour. Allow to cool. 🅣

3. Paint all the dominoes one color. Allow to dry.
4. Print dots in a different color with the blunt end of a pencil, following the patterns below. Allow to dry. 🅗
5. Paint the dominoes all over with glue for a varnish.
6. Learn how to play the game of dominoes (see opposite). 🅗

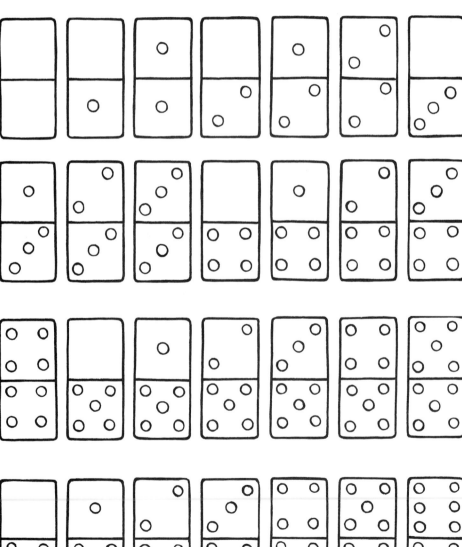

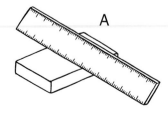

A

To Play Dominoes (Four Players):

1. Spread the dominoes out face down on the table. Each of the four players takes four dominoes.

2. The first player puts a domino face up on the table. The next player must put a matching domino at one end of it, as shown.

3. When a player does not have a domino that matches, he picks up one of those lying face down. If this matches, he can put it down immediately. If not, he keeps it and waits for his next turn.

4. A double domino, with two matching numbers, is placed crosswise. Three more dominoes can be added to it, one in the middle and one at each end.

5. The winner is the first player to put down all his dominoes.

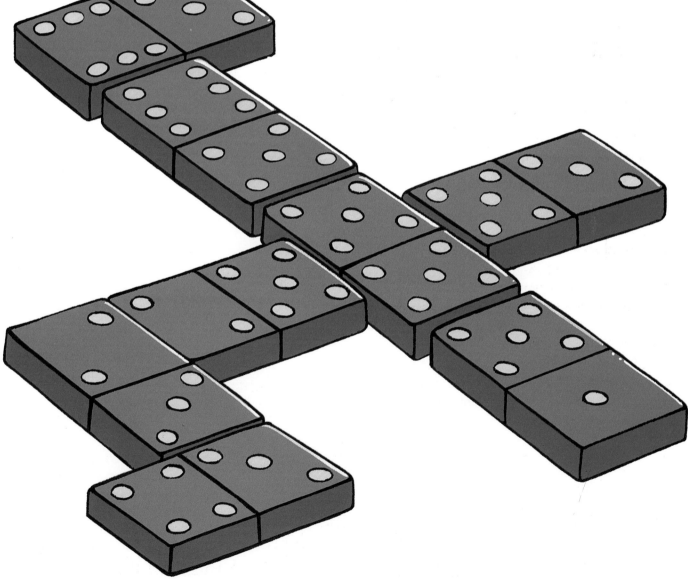

149

Spinner
• • • • • • • • • • •

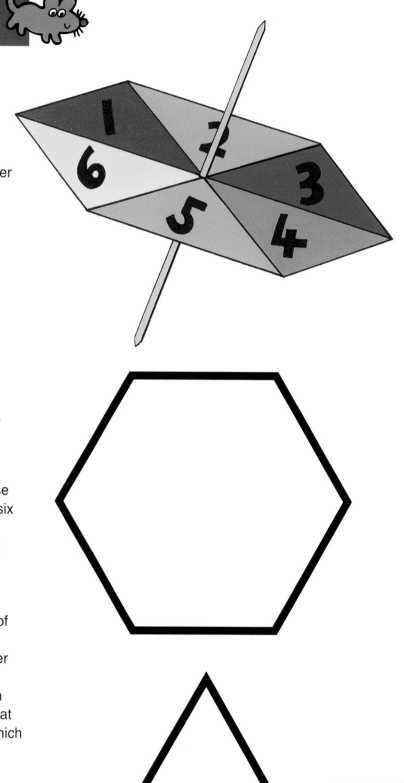

Materials For Each Child:
1/4 sheet of 9" x 12" white construction paper
hexagon and triangle templates, to share
construction-paper scraps in 6 colors
toothpick
small piece of modeling clay
black marker
pencil
scissors
ruler
glue

Class Preparations:
Use the patterns to make hexagon and
triangle templates for the children to share.

Directions:
1. Use a template to trace and cut out a
hexagon from white construction paper. Use
a pencil and ruler to divide the shape into six
triangles, as shown.
2. Use a template to trace and cut out six
paper triangles in different colors. Use a
marker to number the triangles one to six.
Glue them on the hexagon.
3. Push the toothpick through the center of
the spinner, as shown. Mold a small piece
of modeling clay around the toothpick under
the spinner to hold it in place.
4. Use your spinner instead of a die when
you play games. Twist the toothpick on a flat
surface to set the spinner spinning. See which
number lands on the table.

Dice

Materials For Each Child:
self-hardening modeling clay in 2 colors
ruler

Directions:

1. Roll a piece of modeling clay into a ball. Make the ball into a cube by using a ruler to flatten the sides.

2. Make 21 tiny clay balls in a different color. Press the balls on the cube to number the sides one to six. The numbers on opposite sides of the die should always add up to seven. (H)

3. Make another die using the second color to make the cube and the first color to make the dots.

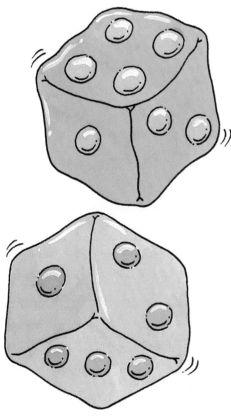

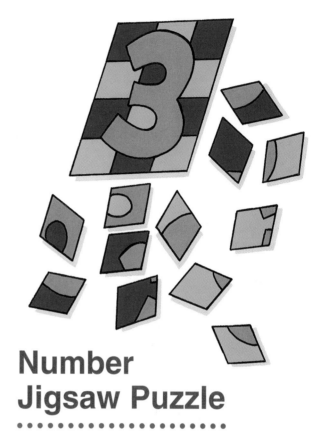

Number Jigsaw Puzzle

Materials For Each Child:
1 sheet of 9" x 12" construction paper
tempera paints in 3 different colors
paintbrush
pencil
scissors
ruler

Directions:

1. Use the pencil and ruler to divide the paper into 12 squares, measuring 3" x 3".

2. Draw a large number between one and nine in the center.

3. Paint the number in one color. Paint the background in two different colors, alternating the color for each square. Allow to dry.

4. Cut the paper along your original pencil lines to make 12 jigsaw-puzzle pieces.

5. Swap puzzles with a friend, and try to put the pieces back together.

Try using bubble-wrap printing to add an extra dimension to paintings with texture.

Bubble Pop Art

Materials For Each Child:
2 sheets of 9" x 12" white or colored construction paper
1 piece of bubble wrap, 9" x 12"
collage materials, such as fabric and paper scraps, yarn, and wiggle eyes
tempera paints and paintbrushes
markers, pencil, scissors, and glue

Class Preparations:
You can adapt this method of printing to fit any theme you desire. You could use it to make frames for the children's artwork (see below). Alternatively, have your students cut shapes from the bubble-wrap printed paper and glue them to a background sheet of paper (see opposite page). Or you could use the printed paper as a background to a collage (see opposite page).

Directions:
1. Paint all over the bumpy side of a piece of bubble wrap. Lay a sheet of construction paper on top and use your hand to gently rub over the back.
2. Peel off the paper and allow the print to dry.
3. Use the bubble-wrap print to make a collage. Add details using markers and collage materials.

Bubble-wrap print used to make frames

Bubble-wrap print used to cut shapes

Bubble-wrap print used as a background

Window Shopping

Materials For Each Child:
1 sheet of 12" x 18" cream construction paper
1 sheet of 9" x 12" brown construction paper
1 sheet of 9" x 12" black construction paper
old magazines and catalogs
colored markers
pencil, ruler, scissors, and glue

Directions:
1. Use a marker to write "Village Store" across the top of a sheet of cream construction paper. Decorate around the shop sign with markers.
2. Cut pieces of brown construction paper, about 1" square, and glue them on the cream paper to make the edge of your shop window.
3. Cut out from old magazines and catalogs pictures of objects that you would like in your shop window. Glue the objects on the paper inside the window.
4. Use a pencil and ruler to measure and cut black construction paper into long strips, about ½" wide. Glue them over the top of the window to make a window frame, as shown below. 🄷

Greek Terracotta Vase

• •

Materials For Each Child:
1 sheet of 9" x 12" black construction paper
clean baby-food jar and newspaper
black and orange or terracotta-colored
    tempera paints and paintbrushes
pencil, scissors, and glue

Class Preparations:
Show the class pictures of ancient Greek pottery.

Directions:
1. Tear newspaper into strips and glue three
layers of strips on the jar, and round the rim.
Allow to dry overnight.
2. Paint the vase orange or a terracotta color.
Allow to dry.
3. Draw and cut out figures and buildings
from black construction paper to decorate your
vase. Try to make them look like the pictures
on ancient Greek vases. Glue the shapes
around the vase.
4. Use black paint to add a border around
the top and bottom of the jar. Allow to dry.
5. Brush with glue to varnish.

Patchwork Pals

• •

Materials For Each Child:
1 sheet of 9" x 12" construction paper in a skin
    tone, with child outline
yarn scraps and glue
colorful fabric scraps
scissors
colored markers

Class Preparations:
Duplicate the pattern on the opposite page
on skin-tone construction paper for each child.

Directions:
1. Cut out the figure. Draw on features
and glue on yarn for hair.
2. Color the T-shirt.
3. Cut a piece of fabric to fit on the pocket.
4. Cut small squares of fabric and glue them
on the dungarees to make a patchwork effect.
5. Glue around the bottom and two sides
of the pocket and stick it on the dungarees.
Then, cut a 1½" square of plain fabric to make
a handkerchief and put it in the pocket.
6. Tape the patchwork pals in a line on the wall.

Use with Patchwork Pals
on page 154.

Pocket

Sailboat Mobile

. . . .

Materials For Each Child:
1 sheet of 9" x 12" brown construction paper,
 with 8 hull outlines
2 sheets of 9" x 12" white construction paper,
 with 4 sail outlines each
4 toothpicks
2 dowels, 12" in length
5 lengths of strong thread
colored markers
scissors, tape, and glue

Class Preparations:
For each child, duplicate the hull pattern on the
opposite page eight times on brown construction
paper and duplicate the sail pattern eight times
on white construction paper.

Directions:
1. Cut out two hulls and two sails for each
boat. Decorate the sails with markers.
2. Glue a toothpick vertically on one boat hull,
as shown (A). Glue another hull on top of the
first, to sandwich the toothpick.
3. Glue the sail onto the toothpick above the
hull (B). Glue another sail on top of the first
to cover the toothpick.
4. Repeat steps 2 and 3 to make three
more boats.
5. To suspend the boats, make a cross with
two dowels and tie them in the center with
thread. Leave a length of excess thread for
hanging the mobile. **H**
6. Tape a piece of thread to each sail, then
tie the other end of the thread to one of the
ends of the crossed dowels. **H**
7. Hang the mobile; then slide the threads
along the crossed dowels to balance the
mobile, if necessary. **T**

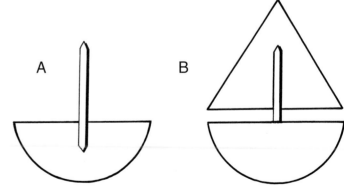

A   B

Finger Puppets

Materials For Each Child:
1/9 sheet of 9" x 12" construction paper
bottle top, to share (optional)
newspaper
tempera paints and paintbrushes
pencil, ruler, scissors, tape, and glue

Class Preparations:
For each child, cut a piece of 3" x 4"
construction paper.

Directions:
1. For each puppet, cut a 3" x 2" strip
of construction paper. Wind it around your
finger to make a tube and tape the side.
2. To make a bird puppet, trace around a
bottle top on construction paper and cut in half
to make a semicircle. Twist it around to make
a cone. Tape the cone to the paper tube to
make a beak, as shown (A). 🖐
3. Tear strips of newspaper and glue them
all over each tube and the cone. Add two
more layers, then leave to dry overnight.
4. Paint the puppets and allow to dry.
Cover with a layer of glue as a varnish.

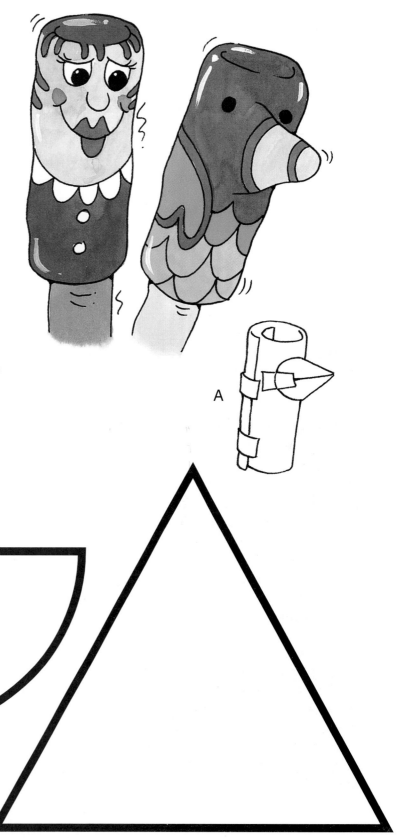

A

Hull

Use with Sailboat Mobile on page 156.

Sail

You could use this collage technique to make a display of different flags from around the world.

Collage Flag

Materials For Four Students:
1 sheet of 12" x 18" blue construction paper, with flag outline
colorful old magazines
gold tempera paint in a shallow dish
pencil and scissors
glue

Class Preparations:
Have the children work in groups of four. Enlarge the flag pattern on the opposite page on a sheet of 12" x 18" blue construction paper for each group.

Directions:
1. Look through the magazines and tear out any pages with plenty of red and white on them.
2. Glue on magazine scraps to fill the seven red stripes and the six white stripes. Allow to dry.
3. Dip the blunt end of a pencil in gold paint and print on the blue rectangle in rows to make 50 stars (or make an old-fashioned flag, with only 13 stars).

Paper-Bead Necklace

Materials For Each Child:
1 piece of colored string, 15" in length
colored construction-paper scraps
skewer
large darning needle
gold paint in shallow dishes

Directions:
1. Tear different-colored construction-paper scraps into seven pieces, approximately 4" x 4".
2. Crumple each piece into a tight, round ball.
3. Roll the ball gently in gold paint, so that the color of the paper still shows. Allow to dry.
4. Use a skewer to make a hole through the center of each ball to make a bead.
5. Thread the needle with string and tie a knot 4" from the end. Thread the beads onto the string, then tie a knot next to the last bead. Tie the ends of the string around your neck to make a necklace.

Use with Collage Flag on
page 158.

anytime

red	white	red	white	red	white	red	white	red	white	red	white	red

white	red	white	red	white	red

Have the children try making different kinds of buildings, such as a skyscraper, a school, or a church.

Paper Bag House

Materials For Each Child:

1 sheet of 12" x 18" brown construction paper
1 brown paper lunch bag
newspaper
paper and tissue-paper scraps
tempera paints
paintbrushes
colored markers
scissors
tape
glue

Directions:

1. Cut off the top of the bag to the height of the building you want to make. Crumple sheets of newspaper and use them to fill the bag. Stick long pieces of tape across the top of the bag to keep the paper in, but try not to squash the bag (A). Turn the bag upside-down for your house.

2. Fold the brown paper in half and cut it to the right width to make a roof. Draw on roof tiles with a marker. Fold over a small flap on each side and spread glue on each flap; then attach the roof to the house (B).

3. Glue on white paper rectangles to represent windows. Crumple colored tissue-paper scraps and glue them along the bottom of the windows for flower boxes. Use paints to add details such as window frames and curtains.

4. Crumple tissue paper to make bushes and glue them to the front and sides of the house.

5. Cut a front door from paper and write a number on it. Fold a flap at one side of the door and glue it to the house so that the door opens. You could draw a person behind the door or draw faces in the windows.

6. Arrange the houses together to make a street. Ⓣ

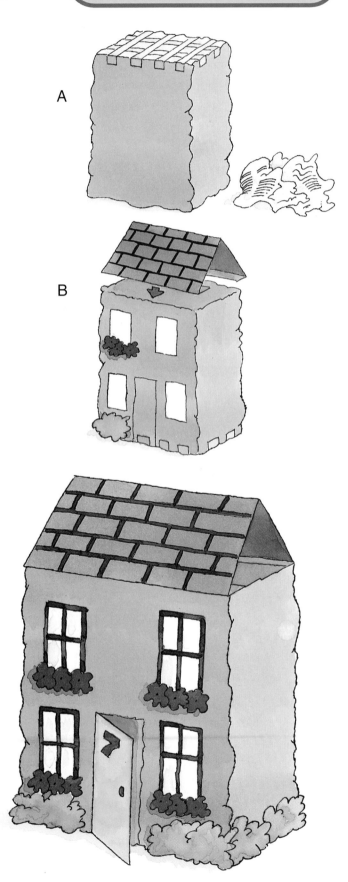

A

B